Plumer & Messines

GENERAL SIR HERBERT CHARLES ONSLOW PLUMER

Plumer & Messines

Accounts of the General and the Battle, 1917

ILLUSTRATED

Sir Charles Harington

Together with
The Third Battle of Ypres by John Buchan &
A Small Biography of General Plumer by Francis
Dodd

LEONAUR

Plumer & Messines
Accounts of the General and the Battle, 1917
by Sir Charles Harington
together with
The Third Battle of Ypres by John Buchan &
A small biography of General Plumer by Francis Dodd

ILLUSTRATED

FIRST EDITION

Leonaur is an imprint of Oakpast Ltd
Copyright in this form © 2023 Oakpast Ltd

ISBN: 978-1-916535-08-4 (hardcover)
ISBN: 978-1-916535-09-1 (softcover)

http://www.leonaur.com

Contents

General Sir Herbert Charles Onslow Plumer, G.C.M.G., G.C.V.O., K.C.B., A.D.C.

By Francis Dodd

Sir Herbert Plumer was born in Devon on March 13th, 1857. In 1876 he entered the York and Lancaster Regiment and served with it in the Soudan War of 1884. In South Africa, in 1896, he raised and commanded a corps of mounted rifles for service in the Matabele rebellion, being mentioned in despatches and receiving the brevet of lieut.-colonel. In the South African War of 1899-1902 he won his first great reputation in the field. He commanded the Rhodesian Field Force and was the first British soldier to cross the enemy frontier.

For months he attempted to reach Mafeking from the north, and, after the happy relief of that historic town, he was one of the most active and resolute of column commanders in the Transvaal. This "small, quiet, resolute man," as a historian describes him, had the power of enforcing discipline and inspiring confidence in the diverse elements under him.

In 1902 he became major-general, and 1908 lieut.-general. In 1904-5 he was Q.M.G. to the Forces and Third Military Member of the Army Council. In 1911-14 he was G.O.C. Northern Command.

Sir Herbert Plumer did not appear in the field in the European War till January, 1915, when he was given command of the new V Corps, holding the southern side of the Ypres Salient.

When General Smith-Dorrien retired in April of that year from the command of the Second Army, Sir Herbert succeeded him. It was that army which fought the Second Battle of Ypres, and has since remained on the left flank of the British front in the West. It has seen severe fighting, such as the Hooge battle of August, 1915, the advance at Hooge during the Battle of Loos in September, 1915, the struggle at the Bluff in the spring of 1916, and the action of the Canadians at Ypres in June of the same year. The Ypres Salient has become historic as the most critical part of the British line.

The Second Army was not engaged during the Battle of the Somme or the first stages of the Battle of Arras, but on Thursday, June 7th, 1917, attacking on the whole front from the Ypres salient to Ploegsteert Wood, it carried all its objectives, with the vital Wytschaete-Messines Ridge, put an end to the embarrassment of the Ypres salient, took over 7,000 prisoners, and accounted for at least 30,000 of the enemy—the whole at a small expense of British lives. The action was probably the most perfectly planned and executed in the history of the campaign.

From Plumer to Messines (Extract)

By Sir Charles Harington

The Northern Command York

The summer of 1914 was ideally beautiful and in July, instead of going up to London for the Eton and Harrow, Sir Herbert Plumer and Lady Plumer motored to the Lakes, making Grasmere their headquarters. The quiet and calm always struck them afterwards as a wonderful preparation for the storm and stress of the Great War which was so soon to break on the world.

On 2nd August the archbishop had a garden party at Bishopthorpe. There was only one thought in everyone's mind. Would there be a war? The archbishop, being told by a person whose opinion he valued that it seemed inevitable, immediately said he would preach in the minster the next day.

It was a wonderful sermon worthy of the occasion which few people who heard it would ever forget.

The next weeks were passed in a fever of preparation. Plumer's Military Secretary, Major Harding Newman, of course gave up his appointment and was in France early in September: his *A.D.C.*, Captain Jones Bateman, rejoined the Norfolk Regiment and gradually most of his staff were replaced by men on the reserve. He longed to go out, but only once did he show even to his wife what he felt, then he said: "You know, if I am not sent out, I send in my papers directly the war is over."

If only those in authority had told him then that, on the death of General Grierson, Sir John French had asked for him, to command the Second Corps, what a difference it would have made to him in those months of waiting and hoping to be sent to the front.

The rumours and scares of invasion were never-ending. Everyone was keen to help, the more uncomfortable the job, the more eager they were to do it.

Sir John Grant Lawson wrote out an appeal for money for the Soldiers' and Sailors' Families' Association, for as all the reservists were called up, their families had to be looked after and provided for. Most generously did Yorkshire respond to the appeal.

Early in November Lord Kitchener, who firmly believed that there would be an attempt made by the Germans to land in the North, ordered the Headquarters to be moved to Newcastle, a most inconvenient arrangement, for there was no place which could be turned into offices, so it meant the general and his staff had to stay at an hotel and go backwards and forwards to the Headquarter Offices in York.

On the 16th November the bombardment of Scarborough and Hartlepool took place. He writes:

Rather an exciting morning as you can imagine. As luck would have it, I had arranged for Chapman to go into York and he had started before I heard anything, so I was alone in the Hotel with telephones going all round. Chapman heard a rumour at Darlington and came straight back. I have sent him to Scarborough and Petrie to West Hartlepool. Scarborough got oft pretty lightly though the Grand Hotel was badly knocked about. Nickalls has been there and returned. There is a lot of damage at Hartlepool, and the number of civilians killed and wounded is pretty heavy—70 killed and 150 wounded. The men (soldiers) behaved very well in both places, and so did the population.

THE FIFTH CORPS

On Christmas Day came a cipher telegram from Lord Kitchener, saying he was to proceed without delay to Belgium to take up the Command of the 5th Corps.

He left on the 5th January. His staff—Jeudwine, Petrie, Brown, Fegan, Stirling, Robertson, Knox, Legge—were all at Southampton and his personal staff consisting of young Heywood and his wife's nephew, Charlie Jackson, were with him.

His one thought when he saw the trenches his men had to occupy was what he could do to better their condition. On 10th January he writes:

> The men are having a very bad time. The mud is awful and the state of the trenches indescribable.

And a week later he writes:

> A nasty cold day, out here one always thinks what it must be for the men in the trenches.

In his Fifth Corps Major-General Snow commanded the 27th Division and Major-General Bulfin the 28th. He writes about some friends who had just lost their sons:

> I am so sorry for them and for all who have lost youngsters who go down every day; it is terrible the number we lose. Colonel Farquhar the C.O. of the Princess Patricia's Canadian Regiment was killed in the trenches at St. Eloi last night, such a gallant fellow and his regiment have done extraordinarily well. It is very trying to have all these good men killed. We lose officers every night and there is no way out of it.

> *April 23rd.* I am writing about 9 a.m. after a very trying night. The French on our left gave way altogether yesterday evening and we were all night in a very awkward position: we still are for that matter, but we are better than we were. I am still all right.

> *April 30th.* The position is very uncomfortable and likely to remain so unless the French make a really serious effort. Things have not been made better by Sir John French slighting Sir Horace, and taking practically all my force

away from him and leaving me independent of him. It is the last thing I wanted. It is not fair because Smith-Dorrien and I were in absolute agreement as to what should be done, and I am only doing now exactly what I should have been doing if I had remained under Smith-Dorrien. He, Smith-Dorrien, feels it very much of course; he came to see me yesterday and had a long talk.

Our casualties have been very heavy and the loss of officers and men is very serious. Three brigadiers have been killed and a great many senior regimental officers. Poor little Burt (York and Lancaster) and his adjutant were both killed, and the regiment have lost heavily, as indeed have nearly all.

It is a depressing statement, but you know how I feel all these losses. On the other hand, the troops without exception have behaved splendidly: they really have done well, and what is so good, is that several of the regiments who did not do so well at the start, have done very well. It has been a pretty severe test to the Northumbrian Division, and they have come out of it well, especially the Northumbrian Brigade. Poor Riddell the brigadier was killed.

On the 6th May, 1915 he was told he was to take over the command of the Second Army. He says in his letter:

I am awfully sorry to leave the corps and the staff. We have gone through some pretty rough times together.

On the 14th May, after the first gas attack, he writes:

When one thinks of all these poor fellows killed and all the sorrow, one feels what a miserable business it is, but we have to go through with it.

When he took over the Second Army Milne was his Chief of Staff, and he was promoted in July and Bruce Williams came in his place. Rycroft was also promoted and Wintour took his place.

In August he got home on leave for five days, and acknowledged that he felt he wanted it, for he was very tired. However, the air at Westgate did him a lot of good and he returned refreshed to his headquarters.

Colonel Wintour, his Chief Administrative Officer, was again ill and had to return to England. Colonel Chichester was appointed in his place.

In November Sir John French told him he was going to recommend him for a "G" and asked which he would prefer, the G.C.B. or G.C.M.G. He chose the latter, which he was given, and also the same month the Legion of Honour and Belgian Order of the Star of Leopold, and his promotion as full general was ante-dated from June.

The second week in December he was told about the change in the Higher Command. On the 22nd December he came on leave for ten days, the longest he had had since the War began.

The health of the troops, which was always one of his chief anxieties, was most satisfactory, and there was a great contrast in numbers between the sick in 1915 and in 1916 over the same period. In 1915, when the army numbered 140,000, they had 10,000 sick, and in 1916, during the same time, when it numbered 260,000 there were only 4,000.

They had a great deal of snow in March and as he puts it in his letter, "the men are having a very bad time in the trenches." There was a good deal of fighting during March. They got back the Bluff, that spot so well known to the Ypres Salient on the 2nd with comparatively little cost.

They had a worrying time about St. Eloi, first the mine exploded and they took 200 prisoners, then in the counter-attack the Germans re-took some of the craters and it was not until the 3rd April that they got them back with some eighty prisoners and part of the line they wanted. Then on the 6th April the Germans re-attacked and the situation was difficult to understand. On the 10th things had improved and the Canadians were holding on. The end of April there was another gas attack.

On the 5th May, 1916 he had the chaplains to tea (27) and spoke to them afterwards; he wrote that it was rather an ordeal.

13

At the end of the month General Bruce Williams was given a brigade and he had to choose a new chief of staff. On the 2nd June I was appointed, but as the Canadians with whom I was then serving, were having such severe fighting I did not actually join the Second Army until the 13th June.

The deaths of so many young men that he knew and who were sons of old friends caused him real sorrow. On 21st July he writes:

Billy Congreve was killed yesterday. It is dreadful; he stood out as one of the youngsters who had done best in the whole force. I feel his death very much. I am just sending you this line to let you know. Poor Walter (Congreve).

MY CHIEF AND HIS METHODS OF COMMAND

It may be of interest to relate the way in which my very happy association with General Sir Herbert Plumer (as he then was) began. I had never met him before the War and the first occasion on which I had that honour was at Trois Tours near Brielen when he visited Major General Baldock, who was then commanding the 49th Division, when I was G.S.O.1. The division was then holding the extreme left of the British Line.

A few days afterwards I was returning from the front line one afternoon when I met an ambulance coming away from Trois Tours and found that Major-General Baldock had been severely wounded in the head at Divisional Headquarters.

He was succeeded by Major-General E. M. Perceval.

Our Headquarters were moved to Hospital Farm near Elverdinghe and it was there that Lord Plumer visited us almost daily.

On one of these visits, I was told that General Plumer had selected me for command of a brigade in the 14th Division at Hooge to replace Brigadier-General Oliver Nugent, as he then was, who was to get a division shortly.

I went home on a week's leave and on my arrival at Boulogne I was told to report at General Headquarters, where I learnt that the late Field-Marshal Sir William Robertson had refused my brigade as he wanted me for Brigadier-General, General Staff of a Corps and I was sent to the Canadian Corps in that capacity on its formation at Bailleul.

I learnt subsequently that I was to have gone to the 12th Corps, destined for Salonika, but owing to Major-General Perceval being in hospital at Hazebrouck with influenza, it was decided to send Brigadier-General Bols to 12th Corps and to keep me for the Canadian Corps. The Canadian Corps was in the Second Army. It moved shortly afterwards up to the Ypres Salient with Headquarters at Abeele. It was commanded, first, by Lieut.-General Alderson and subsequently by General Sir Julian Byng, whom I had never met before.

The Canadians had a lot of hard fighting and were heavily attacked at Mount Sorrel on 3rd June, 1916, and lost Mount Sorrel. This was a severe blow as Sir Douglas Haig was then preparing for the Somme offensive and did not want to spare any troops to come north at the moment. He, however, sent up one 6-in. Howitzer Brigade and on 13th June the Canadians, with the help of that Howitzer Brigade, regained Mount Sorrel.

That was really a magnificent performance and reflected the greatest credit on the Canadian Corps.

It was between 3rd June, and 13th, 1916, that General Byng said to me one day; "You have got to go to the Second Army as Major-General, General Staff."

Knowing his sense of humour, I never took it seriously. I had known that Brigadier-General Bruce Williams was vacating the appointment in order to take up a command, but I had never given a thought to any idea that I should even be considered for such an appointment.

When, however. General Plumer visited our Headquarters next day, I thanked him for his kindness in selecting me. Whereupon, he remarked in a moment, "I won't have you at all unless you get Mount Sorrel back."

At daybreak on 13th June, 1916, the Canadians recaptured Mount Sorrel and I joined the Second Army that day and thus began that happy association, the memory of which is ever sacred to me and which only ended when I followed his remains into Westminster Abbey.

It is quite beyond me to describe what that association has meant to me during these years. I shall, however, I hope, be able to give some picture of what life in that happy Second Army family meant to all of us who were privileged to serve therein and what our chief meant to each one of us.

I like to look back on that 13th June, 1916, when I joined the Second Army Headquarters and General Plumer's own Mess, which consisted of the Chief, his Major-General i/c Administration, Major-General Chichester, Major Knowles, Assistant Military Secretary, and two *aides-de-camp*—Captain Marcus Heywood and Captain Butler.

I was terribly overawed at taking up this new appointment. An army seemed so enormous.

I had never aspired to think in armies. The Canadian Corps had always seemed to be the limit of my horizon and now I found myself confronted by four corps and all the attendant artillery and other services. I had only one asset and that was that I did know the Ypres Salient, having served with the 49th Division and Canadian Corps in every part and I think I knew all the 33 miles of front line which was held by the army at that time.

I was soon to learn something of the chief's methods and to this day I have never failed to try and follow them.

I remember so well just after his brilliant victory of Messines, being asked to what I attributed his success and I replied, "Trust, Training and Thoroughness"—all beginning with a "T." Trust in God and in His Army. He knew the value of Training and left nothing to chance and his Thoroughness was quite remarkable. He took a most active part in the supply and medical arrangements behind his army. No detail escaped him and he spared no effort to see that everything possible was done for those under his command. I remember once asking him how he acquired all his knowledge of administration and detail behind an army. He told me that he owed it all to having been Quartermaster-General of the Army.

I was soon to learn his secret of command. It may well be

summed up as trust. I found myself the first morning at a conference with the army commander. There were also present the Major-General i/c Administration, the Major-General, Royal Artillery, the Major-General, Royal Engineers, the Chief Signal Officer, the Chief Intelligence Officer, the Director-General, Medical Services, the Chief Ordnance Officer, the G.S.O.1, and perhaps one or two others.

Here then was the team through which he worked and this team, which I had just been privileged to join, were in his real confidence. The conference always started by the intelligence officer giving a little summary of the situation on both the British and enemy front, so we all had the same story. Then, we each in turn brought up any points as regards our own branch of the staff and took the chief's orders and decisions and rendered to him an account of our actions during the past twenty-four hours. The great point was that we all knew what every branch was doing and were thus all in the picture.

Those conferences were held every morning at 8.30 a.m., or in winter at 5.30 p.m.

Army Headquarters is a very vast machine and the reader may imagine that the heads of the staff then spent the day in their offices working this big machine. Far from it in the Second Army. We were Plumer's team. We were privileged to know his mind and his wishes and it was our job to carry his spirit of trust and helpfulness to the lower formations in the army—to corps and divisions and below. It was our business to be out helping others with their difficulties.

Directly after the daily conference, the chief with an *aide-de-camp* went off on his rounds. He must have averaged 100 miles a day. I think most of us did. We used to leave with signals our general direction, including some headquarters at which we were certain to call. My tours were generally in the opposite direction to those of the chief in order to visit as many formations as possible, though we would often arrange to meet during the day at some corps headquarters to discuss any problem.

By this means it is fair to say that every corps and divisional headquarters and most brigade headquarters were visited almost daily by either the chief himself or by one of his team and always with the object of ascertaining if there was anything we could do to help. It was by this means that he won the trust and confidence down to brigades, but that was not enough. He had a junior staff officer or liaison officer with each corps whose duty it was to know every battalion and to spend at least two nights a week in the front-line trenches and to know those trenches well by day and night and, further, he instituted courses for commanding officers at our Second Army School.

We had about twelve at a time for about ten days. During which time they could see what went on at various schools and they were all received by the army commander. In addition, this break gave them a useful rest from the line. It is also true to say that hardly a day passed without the chief visiting some unit or units which had just come out of the line and many letters I have received testify to the gratitude and encouragement which he extended to them.

I have written at some length on his methods of command in order to show how he extended his network of trust throughout the whole army. No easy matter and a veritable triumph for the personality of one man.

It is difficult in these days to picture the size of an army. I remember the Second Army on two occasions containing over thirty divisions—some three-quarters of a million men, *i.e.*, five times the size of our original Expeditionary Force.

In his daily tours none were forgotten. One moment he was in the forward area visiting various headquarters the next he was in the back areas saying a kind and encouraging word to men in rest billets or horse lines, visiting gun positions workshops, railheads, hospitals and army schools. He made all realise that they were part of his big machine. He had been a regimental soldier and he never forgot it. He had an intense love and admiration for the British soldier. He impressed on us very firmly that we were nothing but servants of the troops and he never allowed an order to be issued without considering how it would be received by the regimental officer and soldier.

He realised to the full that all depended on the regimental soldier. The best plans, the best orders in the world could easily end in failure unless you had the trust and goodwill of the regimental soldier. Hence no effort was spared to do our best to help those who served in the Second Army.

Those of us who were privileged to serve in his team know well what we owe to him. His own personality so permeated the whole army that our task was made easy. We were also received with trust by all formations They knew that we were his children and brought up on his ideas and that we were a team.

Looking back after all these years, I often wonder why everyone was so good to us and let us go just anywhere we liked without formally visiting the various corps and divisional headquarters *en route,* and, I think it was because they knew that we never carried tales. We were never "spies" or "sneaks." We only existed to help and I think all realised that our chief would never tolerate staff officers who worked on those lines.

The word jealousy never entered into his vocabulary and for that reason every branch of the staff welcomed instead of rejected points raised by any other branch of the staff.

Frequently from my daily tours I would bring back administrative and other points raised by the Royal Artillery, Royal Engineers, Signals, etc., and pass them on to be dealt with and the Major-General i/c Administration and others would bring back General Staff points for me. No idea of resentment ever existed. We were just part of the team and all working for the honour of the Second Army and our chief. It was just a joy to work with men like that.

What I have attempted to describe above has been what I may term his normal method of working in order to carry out his great and responsible task namely the defence of the Ypres Salient.

He realised the conditions under which men had to live and fight to hold that great Trust—the Ypres Salient. His one thought was for his men. He never spared himself in his efforts to do all that was humanly possible for them and it was our privilege to do our best to help him.

Now I come to his method of the preparation of an attack and I will take first of all the preparation of the Battle of Messines, a success to be associated with his name ever after.

The Germans had held the Messines-Wytschaete Ridge ever since 1914. This ridge completely dominated the British trenches and had been a veritable menace to our troops for more than two years.

During 1915 and 1916, plans had been prepared for the capture of this ridge and a number of mines had been prepared under the ridge. It had been the policy of the commander-in-chief to prepare plans to strike either from the north—that is from the Ypres Salient—or from the Somme and the Second and Fourth Armies prepared plans accordingly. The Somme offensive was chosen in 1916 and the other in 1917 I remember so well being with the chief at an Army Commanders' Conference with Sir Douglas Haig, the Commander-in-Chief. That was on 7th May, 1917. Sir Douglas Haig announced that the attack on Messines would be carried out with a view to a further advance to the north-east. Sir Douglas asked our chief when he would be in a position to attack the Messines-Wytschaete Ridge and he replied, "Today month, sir," and it was so. We came back that day full of hope. The Second Army had its chance at last. We were going to bè tried out. It was a wonderful month. Everything we wanted we were given. Almost every day more guns, and more divisions, etc. arrived.

THE BATTLE OF MESSINES

I had not intended in this "*memoir*" to go into much detail of the Battle of Messines, but in view of the fact that attacks have been made on the men who bore the responsibility of command in the late war, I am bound to set forth in greater detail the preparations for that battle.

The following is just a summary of the Messines operations for which I am indebted to the Official Historian:

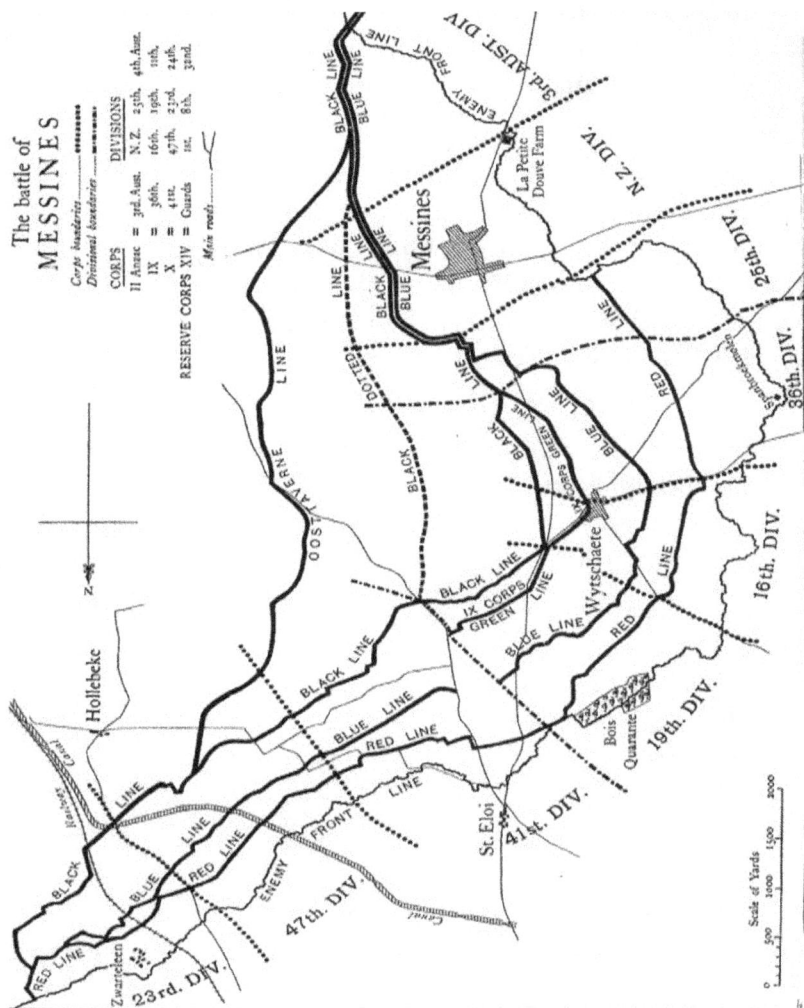

The battle of
MESSINES

Corps boundaries ....
Divisional boundaries ....

CORPS   DIVISIONS
II Anzac = 3rd. Aust.   N.Z. 25th. 4th.Aust.
    IX   = 36th.   16th. 19th. 11th.
    X   = 4th.   47th. 23rd. 24th.
RESERVE CORPS XIV = Guards 1st. 8th. 32nd.

Main roads ....

Hollebeke

Zwarteleen

23rd. DIV.

47th. DIV.

St. Eloi

41st. DIV.

19th. DIV.

Bois Quarante

16th. DIV.

Wytschaete

36th. DIV.

25th. DIV.

Messines

La Petite Douve Farm

N.Z. DIV.

3rd AUST. DIV.

Scale of Yards
0   500 1000 1500 2000

At an Inter-Allied Conference held in Paris on the 4th-5th May, 1917, after the failure of the Nivelle offensive, it was unanimously agreed that:

It was indispensable to continue offensive operations on the Western Front . . . the methods to adopt and put in practice, the choice of the moment and of the place of the different attacks are the business of the generals responsible.

Mr. Lloyd George adding, "the enemy must not be left in peace one moment." Two days later, on the 7th May, at an Army Commanders' Conference at Doullens, Sir Douglas Haig issued his instructions announcing that the main effort would "now be transferred to the north with the ultimate object of securing the Belgian Coast and of obtaining further strategic results." The operations were to be carried out in two phases:

(a) The attack on the Messines-Wytschaete Ridge to secure the right flank for further operations.
(b) "Northern operations" (that is "Passchendaele") a few weeks later, with a view to securing the Belgian Coast.

Sir D. Haig had ever since he became commander-in-chief been in favour of recovering the Messines Ridge, freeing Ypres, and driving the enemy from the coast. Preparation for the first item had been begun as early as June, 1915, and on the 14th January, 1916, within a month of his taking command, he definitely instructed Sir Herbert Plumer to consider, among others, a scheme for an offensive against the ridge.

On the 10th April, after examination of the various schemes, he decided that the preparations for the capture of the ridge should be proceeded with and that mining should be included in them. On the 30th May he warned General Plumer to push on with his preparations with all possible speed as, if the Somme offensive met with considerable opposition, it might be decided to stop it and proceed with the Messines operation. Lack of labour and material made the work of preparation (roads, railways, dumps, etc.) slow, but the majority of the mines were ready by June, 1916.

The troops allotted for the 1917 operations were:

II Anzac Corps: 3rd Australian, New Zealand, 25th and 4th Australian;
IX Corps: 36th, 16th, 19th and 11th Divisions;
X Corps: 41st, 47th, 23rd, 24th Divisions;
Reserve Corps (XIV): Guards, 1st, 8th, 32nd Divisions.

The objectives of the operation were:

(*a*) To capture the enemy position on Messines ridge from St.Yves to Observatory ridge, a front of about 9 miles;
(*b*) to capture as many as possible of the enemy's guns behind the ridge;
(*c*) to consolidate a position to secure possession of the ridge and establish a series of posts in advance.This second objective was subsequently defined as the Oosteraverne line, which stretched like a chord across the base of the Wytschaete salient.

I have mentioned that it was on the 7th May that General Plumer told the commander-in-chief that he would be ready to carry out the attack on the 7th June.

I have before me every order and instruction issued from the 10th May onwards to the corps concerned.

They recall to my memory his most amazing attention to every detail. They recall his conferences with his corps commanders and the decisions taken, the gradual building up of the picture. He knew so well how much depended on the artillery plan. He viewed that from the infantry point of view.Whilst the Infantry were training in back areas or on om model near the Scherpenberg, he was perfecting the artillery arrangements. We actually carried out artillery and machine-gun rehearsals on the enemy.

I extract the following from instructions which I issued on his behalf:

It is of paramount importance that the enemy should be forced to disclose his batteries and that the same should be overpowered before the attack is launched. In order to make his decisions regarding the above it is essential that the army commander should be kept in the closest touch with the opinions of corps commanders regarding:

(*a*) the progress of wire cutting;

(*b*) the progress of destruction;

(*c*) the progress of counter-battery work.

For this purpose, a general staff officer and an artillery staff officer from the army staff will visit corps each afternoon from now onwards to obtain the latest impressions, etc.

So, characteristic of his thoroughness. His infantry were not going to be launched at uncut wire and we had to cut through 280 miles of it.

I quote another extract issued on the 3rd June, 1917, to corps concerned:

The army commander has directed me to bring the following points in connection with today's rehearsals to your notice for necessary action.

(Here follow some technical points about the artillery.)

Reports should be obtained from the *infantry* on the experience of today's rehearsal and a summary thereof forwarded to A.H.Q. The barrage appeared to be thin and was so. It should be explained to the *infantry* that not more than 72% of the guns were firing today as the latest arrivals had not been registered.

I quote that to show his constant thought for the infantry soldier. In all battles it is difficult to settle the exact hour of attack. In this one especially was this the case on account of the mines. A certain time has to be allowed for the falling debris before the Infantry can advance. This required very careful calculation and I have before me the tests carried out by Colonel Mitchell, G.S.O. Intelligence and other staff officers of Second Army H.Q., on days previous to the attack calculating that at

2.45 a.m. a man was just discernible at seventy-five yards' distance—at 3 a.m. at hundred yards etc. That at 2.30 a.m. ground broken with shell-holes could be passed with difficulty and that at 3.15 a.m. irregularities could be easily discerned. That at 2.30 a.m. new wire could be seen one and a half yards away—old rusty wire one yard away, etc. etc.

From these calculations the army commander himself decided that zero hour should be at 3.10 a.m. It makes one wonder whether critics are right when they say that our commanders in the late war were callous of life and that it is hoped that we may be spared from such commanders in the next war. As a story of Messines, I think that I cannot do better than quote from a document entitled *The Battle of Messines*, which I issued in July, 1917. It begins with the following description of the Messines-Wytschaete Ridge:

> The Messines-Wytschaete Ridge, which rises from the River Douve in the south, comprises the plateau, on which are situated the villages of Messines and Wytschaete, and extends northwards by the Damm Strasse (sunken road) to the White Château on the South bank of the Ypres-Comines Canal. The high ground continues North of the canal, through Hill 60, Observatory Ridge and Stirling Castle towards Zonnebeke.
>
> This position, which dominated the Ypres salient, gave to the enemy complete observation of our front system of trenches and forward battery positions, and it had been strongly fortified by the Germans during the two-and-a-half years during which it had been in their possession.

The following is a summary of what happened:

The attack was delivered at 3.10 a.m. on the 7th June.

The nineteen mines on the front of attack, containing 957,000 lb. of explosive, were fired at zero, blowing up large portions of the enemy's front line and support trenches, and causing great demoralisation and loss of the garrisons of the trenches.

The artillery barrage opened simultaneously, and the infantry advanced to the assault after the debris and shock of the mines had subsided.

Previous to the day of attack, six brigades, R.F.A., five 6-in. howitzer batteries and a 60-pdr. battery had been placed in action as far forward as possible without being actually in view. These batteries did not open fire till zero hour.

Owing to the previous effective wire cutting and trench bombardment, the infantry were able to carry the whole of the enemy's front-line system within a few minutes. Following closely the artillery barrage, our troops pressed on up the western slopes of the ridge with scarcely a pause, and within three hours of the commencement of the attack had stormed the crest of the ridge along the whole front of the attack.

The garrisons of the village of Wytschaete and the White Château, south of the Ypres-Comines Canal, held out for some time, but their resistance was overcome by the attacking waves of infantry, and by 10 a.m. the objective line, East of Messines-Wytschaete, the Damm Strasse and Hill 60, had been captured by the assaulting troops. Only in one locality in Battle Wood, north of the Ypres-Comines Canal, did the enemy continue to offer resistance.

Tanks were started from behind the infantry assembly trenches and followed the infantry advance; the success of the infantry, however, did not afford many opportunities for effective action by tanks before the first objective lines had been gained. Fifteen out of forty tanks were able to reach their objectives near the Damm Strass and east of Wytschaete, and afforded moral, as well as material, support, besides drawing on themselves hostile fire which would otherwise have been directed against the infantry.

A halt was made on the objective line east of Messines and Wytschaete for about five hours, during which the captured position was reconnoitred by the attacking troops and the work of consolidation was commenced. During this interval infantry and cavalry patrols pushed forward in advance, supported by tanks, in order to prevent the enemy removing guns and to clear the ground to the east of Wytschaete for the further advance.

Before the attack on the Oosttaverne Line began, some forty batteries of field artillery and several sections of 6-in. howitzers and 60-pdrs. had moved to previously selected forward positions for the more effective support of the operation. These were chiefly from the centre corps, whose objective had the greatest depth.

About 2.30 p.m. the enemy attempted to launch a local counter-attack just north and south of Messines, but was driven back by our artillery, rifle and Lewis-gun fire.

At 3.10 p.m. a further advance was made against the Oosttaverne Line by fresh troops supported by tanks, which had been brought forward after the line east of Messines and Wytschaete had been captured. These troops advanced through the original assaulting columns and pushed down the eastern slopes of the ridge. Within an hour the Oosttaverne Line had been captured with the exception of a small portion east of Messines, which fell into our hands on the following morning.

During the evening of the 7th June another local counter-attack was delivered by the enemy east of Messines, but failed to drive back our troops.

The brunt of our attack fell on the 2nd (Prussian) Division, the 35th (Prussian) Division, the 40th (Saxon) Division and the 3rd (Bavarian) Division: the latter division being involved in a relief of the 40th (Saxon) Division when the attack commenced.

These four enemy divisions suffered great losses, both in casualties and prisoners, and were withdrawn from action, taking no further part in the subsequent fighting.

The 204th (Württemberg) Division and the 4th (Bavarian) Division on the flanks also suffered heavy losses.

The 1st Guard Reserve Division was brought forward on the evening of the 7th June to relieve the 3rd (Bavarian) Division and delivered the second unsuccessful counter-attack.

During the night of the 7th-8th June our troops established themselves in positions;

(*a*) On the main line of defence east of Messines and Wytschaete;

27

(*b*) On the advanced position in the Oosttaverne Line.

The work of consolidation was carried out by the troops who had captured the positions, and, in the meantime, additional field-artillery batteries, 60-pdr. batteries and 6-in. howitzer batteries were pushed forward to the eastern slopes of the ridge so as to bring fire to bear at closer range covering our new positions.

On the evening of the 8th June the enemy delivered a strong counter-attack against the whole front of attack after a heavy bombardment, but was unable to penetrate our advanced positions at any point.

At least three enemy divisions—the 7th Division, 24th (Saxon) Division, 1st Guard Reserve Division—and portions of the 4th (Bavarian) and 16th (Bavarian) Divisions took part in this counter-attack, but were unable to make any progress in the face of artillery, machine-gun and rifle fire.

After the 8th June patrols were sent forward by us from the Oosttaverne Line and advanced posts established at various points.

Our positions were strengthened, artillery moved forward, roads opened up, signal communications established, light railways and water-supply systems extended to forward positions.

On the 11th June the enemy's positions in the vicinity of the Potterie Farm, south-east of Messines, were captured, which deprived him of a fortified locality, with communication trenches to Warneton, in which he had been able to organise local counter-attacks against our positions near Messines.

On the 12th June the enemy was suspected of withdrawing from his front line between the River Lys and the right of our new position south of Messines. Reconnaissances by patrols and air reconnaissances confirmed this movement subsequently.

On the 14th June a further advance was made along the whole front, and new line established, covering the crossings of the River Lys as far as Warneton on the south, and clearing up the situation in Battle Wood, north of the Ypres— Comines Canal.

The enemy offered no serious resistance to this further advance.

The success of the operations may be attributed to:

(a) The exceptionally good counter-battery work, trench bombardment, wire cutting, and barrage work by the artillery.

(b) The determination and valour of the assaulting infantry, who were animated by a splendid fighting spirit.

(c) The fine work of the Flying Corps, who allowed nothing to deter them from the effective execution of the tasks allotted to them.

(d) Good Staff work, not only in the previous preparations, but also in the co-ordination of the work of the various arms during the operations.

(e) The systematic training of all troops beforehand, so that all ranks were aware of the tasks which they had to carry out and the ground over which they would have to work.

(f) The careful preparation of the administrative arrangements for railways, roads, water supply, ammunition supply, etc.

(g) The successful explosion of the mines.

On the other hand, the causes which led to the enemy's defeat may be summarised as follows:

(a) The date and hour of the attack do not appear to have been anticipated, although he was well aware of the impending attack and approximately the front on which it could be expected.

(b) His troops in the line were exhausted by the artillery preparation, which not only lowered their morale, but also prevented rations and water reaching them during the last few days.

(c) The destruction of his artillery in the Oosttaverne Group which prevented effective artillery support being given to his infantry when the attack was launched.

(d) The use of gas projectiles and gas projectors which

caused casualties and constant precautions against this form of attack.

(*e*) The demoralisation of the troops holding the front and support trenches, caused by the mine explosions.

The total number of prisoners captured during the operations from 1st to 20th June amounted to 7,261, including 150 officers; while 51 guns, 242 machine guns, and 60 trench mortars, fell into our hands.

I append a copy of messages received from His Majesty the King and H.R.H. the Duke of Connaught and also the Special Order of the Day issued by the commander-in-chief.

The following telegrams are published for the information of all ranks:

To Field-Marshal Sir Douglas Haig,
from His Majesty the King.

9.6.17

I rejoice that, thanks to thorough preparation and splendid co-operation of all arms the important Messines Ridge, which has been the scene of so many memorable struggles, is again in our hands. Tell General Plumer and the Second Army how proud we are of this achievement by which, in a few hours, the enemy was driven out of strongly entrenched position held by him for two-and-a-half years.

From Field-Marshal Sir Douglas Haig,
to His Majesty the King.

9.6.17

Your Majesty's gracious message has been read with intense pride and gratification by all who have taken part in the operations on the Messines Ridge.

In the name of myself and staff, General Plumer and all ranks of the Second Army, I beg to offer our respectful thanks to Your Majesty.

(Signed)   D, Haig, F.M.
C.-in-C., British Armies in France.

30

General Sir Herbert Plumer.

As an old chief of yours may I offer you and your army my congratulations on your splendid success and am glad to hear your losses have not been too heavy.

Connaught.

ORDER OF THE DAY.

The complete success of the attack made yesterday by the Second Army under the command of General Sir Herbert Plumer is an earnest of the eventual final victory of the Allied cause.

The position assaulted was one of very great natural strength, on the defences of which the enemy had laboured incessantly for nearly three years. Its possession overlooking the whole of the Ypres Salient was of the greatest tactical and strategical value to the enemy.

The excellent observation which he had from this position added enormously to the difficulty of our preparations for the attack and ensured to him ample warning of our intentions. He was therefore fully prepared for our assault and had brought up reinforcements of men and guns to meet it.

He had the further advantage of the experience gained by him from many previous defeats in battles such as the Somme, the Ancre, Arras and Vimy Ridge. On the lessons to be drawn from these he had issued carefully thought-out instructions.

Despite all these advantages the enemy has been completely defeated. Within the space of a few hours all our objectives were gained, with undoubtedly very severe loss to the Germans. Our own casualties were, for a battle of such magnitude, most gratifyingly light.

The full effect of this victory cannot be estimated yet, but that it will be very great is certain.

Following on the great successes already gained it affords final and conclusive proof that neither strength of position nor knowledge of and timely preparation to meet impending assault can save the enemy from complete defeat, and that, brave and tenacious as the German troops are, it is only a question of how much longer they can endure the repetition of such blows.

Yesterday's victory was due to causes which always have given and always will give success, *viz*.: the utmost skill, valour and determination in the execution of the attack following on the greatest forethought and thoroughness in preparation for it.

I desire to place on record here my deep appreciation of the splendid work done, above and below ground as well as in the air, by all army, services, and departments, and by the commanders and staffs by whom, under Sir Herbert Plumer's orders, all means at our disposal were combined, both in preparation and in execution, with a skill, devotion and bravery beyond all praise.

The great success gained has brought us a long step nearer to the final, victorious, end of the war, and the Empire will be justly proud of the troops who have added such fresh lustre to its arms.

D. Haig,
Field–Marshal,
Commanding–in–Chief,
British Armies in France.

Adv. G.H.Q.
8th June, 1917.

Before leaving Messines, it might be of interest to my readers if I gave a short account of how my chief set about preparing for the Messines operations which he carried through so successfully.

His first object was to settle the plan. This he did by conferences with his corps commanders and they in turn with their divisional commanders. The latter, no doubt, adopted the same course with their brigade commanders. The greatest difficulty in the preparation of an attack in static warfare is;

(*a*) To settle the main objective.

(*b*) To settle the various stages towards getting it.

(*c*) To settle the line of attack.

(*d*) To settle the pace of the barrage.

These are matters on which those concerned never agree.

It is interesting, therefore, to relate how he dealt with them. The answer really is by personal contact with the commanders concerned.

He held conferences at various corps headquarters so as to save the corps commanders coming up to Cassel. He visited divisional and brigade commanders daily and discovered their plans and got their ideas. We all did the same in order to help them and keep them in the whole picture and thus, when the orders were finally issued, every commander felt that he had at any rate been consulted and had had his way and had talked personally to the chief. He might not agree as to the pace of the barrage or the hour of attack, but anyhow he had been asked. All cheerfully accepted the final decision and put their best into it.

Similarly, the major-general, Royal Artillery, kept them informed of the intensive artillery support they were going to receive, the greatest concentration in the whole War. And in addition, a huge model of the Messines-Wytschaete Ridge was constructed near The Scherpenberg. It was about the size of two croquet lawns. On this all those taking part down to Platoon Commanders were able to study the ground.

It was a wonderful study of human nature. He treated the whole army as a family. He took them all into his confidence and trusted them. They trusted him and that army went into the Battle of Messines in great heart knowing that their chief had done everything possible for them.

I quote the above, as I fear there were instances in the war of the reverse of the picture. When lower formations were not consulted but merely ordered into action with the result that they thought that neither the stages, nor the time of attack, nor the pace of the barrage was correct, and, therefore, did not start in good heart. Simply the difference between the art of commanding by trust as against distrust.

What, however, I have written so far regarding Messines has had all to do with the battle plans. No one realised more fully than my chief the fact that the most brilliant plans depend for success on what happens behind and that was where his great knowledge of organisation came in. The days he spent siting railheads, dumps, etc., with the Major General i/c Administration, or gun positions and railways to them with the major-general, Royal Artillery. Hospitals, etc., with the Director General Medical Services. Signal communications with the chief signal officer. Repair shops, etc., with the chief ordnance officer. Engineering works and roads with the major-general, Royal Engineers. Mining detail with the officer i/c mines. The tank programme with the officer commanding tanks. Air photographs and intelligence with the general staff officer (intelligence). The air programme with the officer commanding, air wing. Every detail of the artillery preparations with the major-general, Royal Artillery.

Units training for the attack in back areas were visited by him.

Nothing whatever was left to chance. He kept his finger on every pulse and the whole army knew it.

Each morning during that month the picture was being fitted in. Our daily conferences were of intense interest, when we were each able to report how the various tasks were progressing.

In my position as Major-General, General Staff, of the Army, I visited the brigadier-generals, general staff of corps daily and found the same enthusiasm in all their preparations and used to return at night to tell the Chief that all appeared to be going well.

About this time our head intelligence officer, Colonel C. H. Mitchell (Canadian Corps), evolved a system of having a sausage balloon behind each corps all connected to a forward report centre at Locre, which would be connected by telephone to my office at army headquarters at Cassel and by which I should be in instant communication with the progress of the battle on each corps front. It was very ingenious and included information from O.P.'s, sound ranging, flash spotting, directional wireless, message dropping from aeroplanes, etc.

I also during this time attended the conferences of the major-general, Royal Artillery, with all his artillery commanders and listened with interest to the preparations to launch the biggest concentration of artillery in history. The preparation of that artillery plan was a fine bit of work and reflected much credit on the M.G.R.A. and the artillery commanders.

I have tried to give a picture of how our chief built up the operation of Messines in every detail and how he worked the whole army as a family and it is interesting to note that the final orders for the Battle of Messines did not cover half a sheet of foolscap.

Everyone knew his job and only wanted an order when to start.

I remember so well on the day before the battle, namely, 6th June, 1917. I was rung up by General Headquarters to say that they were sending up the whole of the press correspondents to see the battle and asking me to give them any information I thought fit. I recollect how these gentlemen, whom I had never met before, arrived at Cassel about 5 p.m. They included Perry Robinson, of *The Times*, Philip Gibbs, Beach Thomas, Herbert Russell and others. I received them all and, having put them on their honour, I told them the whole plan for the morrow and told them if they came back at 5 p.m. the following day that I would tell them how much of the plan we had been able to accomplish.

It was with no little pride that I was able to tell them that our beloved chief had succeeded in taking every objective and at a cost of one-fifth of the casualties we had anticipated.

I treasure greatly an album presented to me by those war correspondents containing cuttings from their various newspapers on the Battle of Messines. This was given me in recognition of the confidence I placed in them in giving them our plans.

How well I remember the eve of Messines. For the first time in my life, I went to bed at 9 p.m. There was nothing more I could do. The troops were then on the move. Zero was at 3.10 a.m. We all had breakfast at 2.30 a.m. with the army commander. The rest of us went to the top of Cassel Hill to see the mines go up. Five hundred tons of explosive. I can see the glow in the sky as I write. Not so the army commander. He was kneeling by his bedside praying for those gallant officers and men who were at that moment attacking.

After that he was with me in my office as news began to come in from our forward report centre—news from our sausage balloons—an eye-witness account such as we are now accustomed to on the wireless. All was going well. The first objective gained—on they all went to the second objective—The Messines-Wytschaete Ridge was ours. I can feel his hand on my shoulder now as the news came through. There were tears in his eyes. He was thinking of those glorious men who had done it. Could we hold it? What about the enemy counter-attack?

At this moment there were reports of an enemy counter-attack from the direction of Warneton. We had three mines at the front edge of Ploegsteert Wood which we had purposely not blown as being outside our attack. If the counter-attack from Warneton developed it would pass over those mines. I got in touch with our officer i/c mines and deliberately planned to blow those mines as the counter-attack passed over them. It would have been terrible and I hated the idea, but I suppose it was war. I was very glad that the counter-attack never materialised.

Another incident occurred when we were in that room. A tank of ours was disabled on the top of the Messines-Wytschaete Ridge and the sausage balloon reported that it was being heavily shelled from a battery which they could see and of which they could give the location. In a moment I was able to tell our wing commander. In thirteen minutes that battery was bombed and silenced and our tank escaped.

It was a great relief that night when we heard that we were firmly established and that the enemy showed no signs of attacking.

It always interests me as I do not think anyone from the army commander downwards ever thought that we were undertaking an operation which would be welcomed and appraised as it was. It never even occurred to me. I knew that we were carrying out a well-prepared task on a limited objective and that was all. I think the army commander was equally bewildered by the telegrams of congratulations which he received on every side.

I went over the ridge next morning, partly by tank, and I shall never forget the sight. I remember so well going into a concrete dug-out near Spanbrookmolen—our biggest crater—and finding four German officers sitting round a table—all dead—killed by shock. They might have been playing bridge. It was an uncanny sight—not a mark on any of them. I can see their ghastly white faces as I write. In the wallet of one of them was found a copy of a message sent at 2.40 a.m.—30 minutes before zero—saying "Situation comparatively quiet."

Standing on the ridge and looking back at what had been the British line for all that time, one wondered how the British soldier had existed. The only answer to that is no one but the British soldier could have existed. I have been there many times since. I still marvel at it all.

And so ended the Battle of Messines—planned—supervised in every detail by our great chief, carried out by his devoted army.

His staff a family, his army a family. All rejoicing that the father of the family had gained such a splendid success.

The situation with the Messines Ridge in our hands was very different as regards the comfort of the troops.

Nothing but ruins remained of the villages of Messines and Wytschaete. We recovered the bell of Wytschaete Church and I was present with the army commander when he restored it to the late King of the Belgians, a very simple but impressive ceremony.

About this time both His Majesty the King and His Royal Highness the Duke of Connaught visited the Messines Ridge. Two of His Majesty's Staff were actually examining the signpost at Wyschaete cross-roads when the enemy topped some heavy stuff there. They fortunately escaped and had to rejoin the party at top speed, much to the king's amusement.

The king spent a few days in a *château* at Cassel and made an extensive tour of the army area, which was much appreciated.

The next few months were spent in preparation for the capture of Passchendaele.

The Part Played by the Second Army in the Passchendaele Operations

Before writing the story of Passchendaele from the Second Army point of view, I want to make it clear to my readers that I am not writing the history of that fighting. That will be done by the official historian. Neither am I writing, as others have done since the war, with a knowledge of both sides, which makes it easy to criticize, especially when those who shouldered the burden and responsibility have been taken from us. I am merely concerned in trying to give a true picture of my old chief facing the tasks with which he was confronted. It is, therefore, fortunate that, as I write, I have before me the following documents:

(*a*) Intelligence summaries and appreciations showing exactly what we knew of the enemy in front of us. His units, gun positions, dumps, reserves. Headquarters, etc.

(*b*) The Second Army orders for every operation up to the capture of Passchendaele.

(*c*) A summary of how and by whom each operation was carried out and the results attained.

All the above were compiled by the Second Army Staff and were signed and issued by myself as secret documents with the approval of the army commander. They admit of no dispute. They are the evidence by which my chief's reputation as regards Passchendaele stands or falls.

I ask my readers to picture him faced with the task entrusted to him by his commander-in-chief, entrusted also with the command at times of some three-quarters of a million men, studying every fraction of information regarding the enemy over the hill, sparing no effort to ensure that his army should be engaged under the best available conditions. On his decision and by his command the orders referred to above were issued.

It is easy to criticize when from German and other writers one knows now the picture of what was the other side of the hill. To discover that was the problem facing those in High Command. We, as his staff, could but compile and put before him what we believed to be the enemy situation after carefully weighing the value of our information. In many cases, no doubt, it was inaccurate. In many cases, no doubt, the enemy information regarding our positions was inaccurate. We were only human.

Our British commanders have been subjected in many quarters since the war to such unfair criticism that I want again, before telling the Second Army story of Passchendaele to picture the army commander, the man who had held the Ypres Salient for two years at that time against many odds, tackling this difficult problem. If I can show my readers that in his plans and arrangements he did everything humanly possible for the men he loved, before he committed them to that task, from which so many never came back, then I venture to hope that his characteristics of loyalty, thoroughness and devotion to duty may be still further enhanced.

The capture of the Messines–Wytschaete Ridge in June, 1917, had prepared the way for the second or northern part of Sir Douglas Haig's programme of advancing north-east to secure the Belgian Coast.

I may say that it was Sir D. Haig's original intention that the northern portion of the attack should be entrusted to the Fourth Army under the late General Sir H. Rawlinson, as both he and his chief staff officer, General Sir A. A. Montgomery Massingberd (now C.I.G.S.), came up to stay with General Plumer in order to reconnoitre the ground and we always thought that the capture of the Passchendaele-Staden Ridge and the subsequent advance towards Bruges and the coast, was to be a combined operation by the Second and Fourth Armies.

This was, however, altered and we received instructions from

1. Cheddar Villa
2. Morteldje Estaminet
3. Hampshire Farm
4. Cross Roads Farm
5. Hill Top Farm
6. The Mound
7. Birr Cross Roads
8. Leinster Farm
9. Halfway House
10. Stirling Castle
11. Clapham Junction
12. Inverness Copse
13. Fitzclarence's Farm
14. Bodmin Copse
15. Maple Copse
16. Observatory Wood
17. Armagh House
18. The Caterpillar
19. Northampton Farm

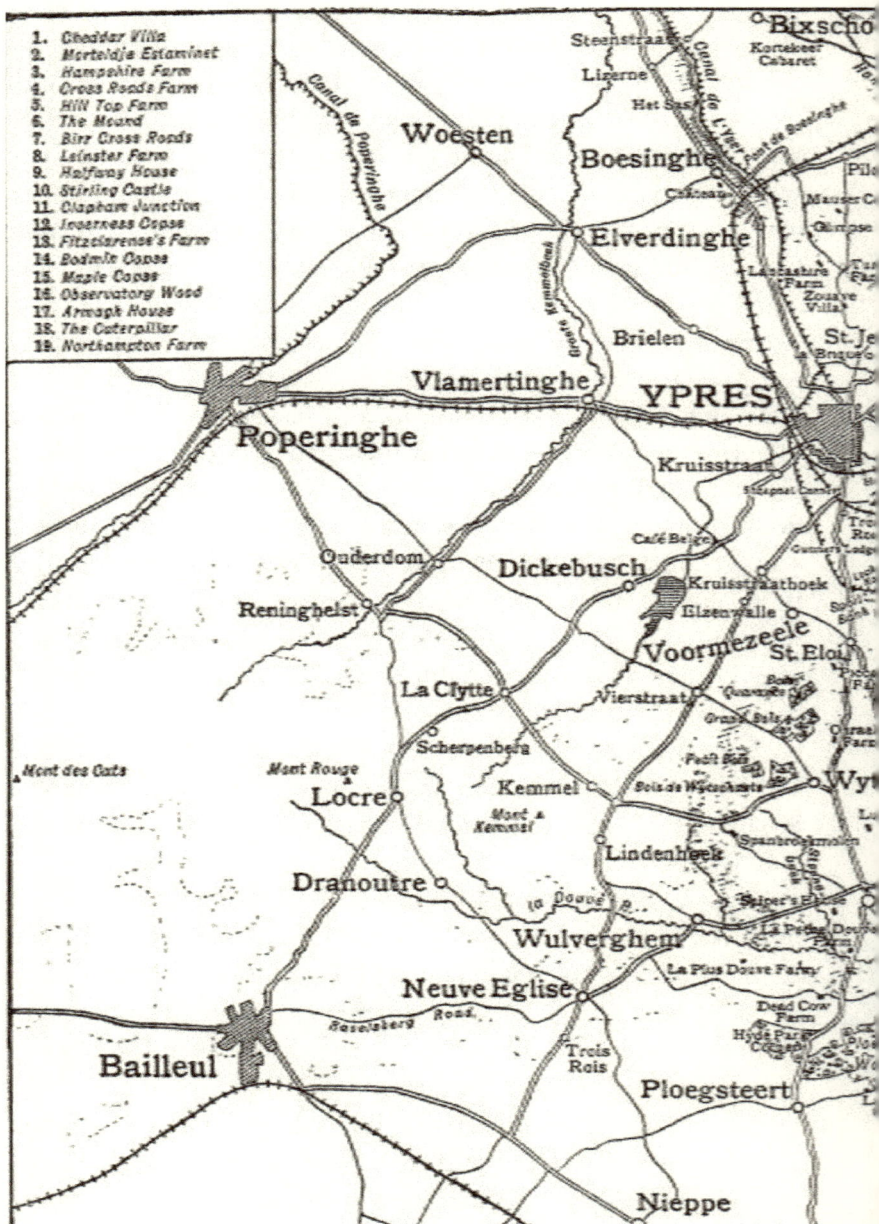

Bixscho
Steenstraat
Kortekeer Cabaret
Lizerne
Canal de l'Yser
Pont de Boesinghe
Het Sas
Woesten
Boesinghe
Pile
Château
Mauser C
Canal de Poperinghe
Elverdinghe
Glimose
Lancashire Farm
Zouave Villa
Brielen
St. Je
Groote Kemmelbeek
Vlamertinghe
YPRES
Poperinghe
Kruisstraat
Café Belge
Dickebusch
Kruisstraatboek
Ouderdom
Reninghelst
Elzenwalle
Voormezeele
St. Eloi
La Clytte
Vierstraat
Mont des Cats
Mont Rouge
Scherpenberg
Kemmel
Bois de Wytschaete
Wy
Locre
Mont Kemmel
Lindenhoek
Spanbroekmolen
Dranoutre
la Douve R.
Wulverghem
La Plus Douve Farm
Neuve Eglise
Ravelsberg Road
Dead Cow Farm
Hyde Park
Bailleul
Trois Rois
Ploegsteert
Nieppe

THE YPRES SALIENT
1914-1918

G.H.Q. that the first stage would be the capture of the Pass-chendaele-Staden Ridge. After this had been secured Sir D. Haig hoped to secure the line approximately Thorout-Couckerlaere and to co-operate with the Fourth Army (General Sir Henry Rawlinson) which had been assembled near the Coast, and also with the navy. Their object was to capture Nieuport and the coast to the east of it. For this object thirty-four British and six French divisions were collected.

The main attack was to be made in the centre by the Fifth Army (General Sir H. Gough) on a seven-mile front Hooge-Pilkem with ten of its sixteen divisions.

The Second Army (General Sir H. Plumer) was to cover its right on a six-mile front with five of its thirteen divisions. The army boundary ran between Zillebeke and Hollebeke. The French First Army (General Anthoine) was to attack on the left of the Fifth Army with two of its six divisions.

General Sir H. Rawlinson's Fourth Army (four divisions) had been secretly collected near the Coast with the object of co-operating with the navy after the main attack had secured the Passchendaele-Staden Ridge.

The plan was quite clear. The capture of the Messines Ridge had made it possible and it certainly appeared to us that the capture of the Passchendaele-Staden Ridge would give us the jumping-off ground from which to prepare for the further advance outlined above.

It was, I understand, all important at that time to draw pressure away from the main French Army. This plan was certain to achieve that result. Sir Douglas Haig warned us in a memorandum on 30th June shortly after Messines that the fundamental object on the operations was the defeat of the German Army and that this could not be achieved in a single battle and that we must make preparations for "very hard fighting lasting perhaps for weeks" and that we must arrange to deliver a series of organised attacks on a large scale and on broad frontages.

I say without any hesitation that my chief, General Sir H. Plumer, welcomed and endorsed the plan. He had known what it was to have his troops sitting day after day and winter after winter under the Messines-Wytschaete Ridge and in front of Ypres, with the enemy holding all the commanding ground. The capture of Broodseinde, Passchendaele, Westroosebeek, Staden was the only solution to the holding of the Ypres Salient and the Germans knew it only too well.

Some writers have been kind enough to describe the capture of the Messines Ridge as a life-saving operation as the casualties were only a fifth of what we feared and it certainly did put an end to an intolerable situation. At the same time, I venture to think that if it had not been for the appalling conditions of weather and mud, which I shall refer to later, the capture of the abovementioned line would have taken us a long way on the road to final victory. In all the painful and bitter criticisms which I have read charging our great commanders with not having abandoned the plans on account of weather and mud, I have not met one who has been bold enough to suggest a line on which we "could" have remained for the coming winter. Lines on maps are very easy things to draw. Lines on the ground where troops can live under the muzzles of enemy rifle, machine and gun fire are very hard to find.

I am not writing without personal knowledge of the actual conditions both of the weather and of the ground at that time. Just after our capture of the Broodseinde Ridge on 4th October, I reconnoitred the Bellevue position under the most appalling conditions prior to the attack of 12th October. It has been said that it was between the above dates that Sir Douglas Haig should have abandoned all further operations. On that I can make no criticism. I was not in a position to know the various factors which influenced him. I certainly never heard the question either raised or mentioned.

Most of the conferences during that period of the Passchendaele fighting between August and November, of Sir Douglas Haig and his army commanders (Generals Plumer and Gough), were held actually in my own office over my own map. One writer has stated that my chief was always opposed to the Passchendaele operations and urged Sir Douglas Haig to abandon them and also that he is reported to have written a letter opposing or throwing cold water on the whole operations. Furthermore, it has been said that my chief told the writer on our way through Paris to Italy that he was very glad to get away from the Western Front.

Few staff officers, I am sure in history, have been so privileged to share the innermost thoughts and actions of their chief as I was and the matters, I have been forced to mention above are just "unthinkable." To enforce this point, I must mention the fact that during the whole period during which I was privileged to serve him I only recollect his writing three official documents himself—one was a telegram from Italy. The other two were telegrams—one to the prime minister and the other to the Secretary of State for War—from Constantinople concerning the situation at the time of Chanak when he came up to pay me a visit and to help his old staff officer.

He always stated his views quite clearly and then trusted me to prepare a draft for his approval or otherwise. It is, therefore, inconceivable to me that his agreement with the views of the commander-in-chief was anything but one of "*utter loyalty*" and desire to carry out his chief's orders to capture Passchendaele. He knew well what that ridge would mean to his beloved troops and I am sure that once within grasp, as it was after his successful capture of the Broodseinde Ridge on 4th October, he never gave a thought to stopping and turning back. I am sure that all the Second Army Staff, who were privileged with me to serve him, will support that statement, and also the fact that no one hated being sent to Italy and leaving the Ypres Salient, which he had held for so long, more than our chief.

No one was more delighted to return to it in the following March than he was. I said earlier that I had studied that ground in front of Passchendaele. I have studied it since both from where our line was on 4th October and from the Passchendaele-Staden Ridge. I still ask the critics to state where our advanced troops could have spent the winter of 1917.

In theory anywhere. In practice nowhere. We find these convenient lines in war games but not in war. I have knelt in the Tynecot Cemetery below Passchendaele on that hallowed ground, the most beautiful and sacred place I know in this world, I have prayed in that cemetery oppressed with fear lest even one of those gallant comrades should have lost his life owing to any fault or neglect on the part of myself and the Second Army Staff. It is a fearful responsibility to have been the one who signed and issued all the Second Army orders for those operations. All I can truthfully say is that we did our utmost. We could not have done more. History must give its verdict. I do not for one moment contend that we did not make mistakes and many of them, and as I read through these old orders before me, I keep recalling the old problems with which we were faced.

Further Details of the Passchendaele Operations

As I said before, I had not intended to go into much detail regarding the Battle of Messines and the same applies to Passchendaele. The latter, however, having recently become the subject of severe criticism, I am in the following chapter giving a summary of those operations, compiled partly with the help of the official historian and partly from memoranda issued by the Second Army Staff at the time. As regards the part played by the Second Army, therefore, these are the official records issued and approved by the commander of the Second Army. No doubt similar records of the part played by the Fifth Army exist and these presumably will be at the service of the official historian when the official account of the Passchendaele operations is written.

The Official Battle Nomenclature divided the fighting in the Battles of Ypres 1917 (21st July-10th November) into eight phases:

(1) The Battle of Pilckem Ridge, 31st July2nd August, with the subsequent "Capture of Westhoek," 10th August.

(2) The Battle of Langemarck, 16th-18th August.

(3) The Battle of the Menin Road, 20th-25th September.

(4) The Battle of Polygon Wood, 26th September–3rd October.
(5) The Battle of Broodseinde, 4th October.
(6) The Battle of Poelcappelle, 9th October.
(7) The First Battle of Passchendaele, 12th October.
(8) The Second Battle of Passchendaele, 26th October–10th November.

The bombardment was begun on the 15th July and gradually intensified, whilst the Royal Flying Corps practically obtained command of the air.

The 25th July was fixed for the date of the first attack, but owing to weather conditions it was postponed to the 28th, and then, at the earnest request of General Anthoine, whose artillery had not produced sufficient effect, to the 31st. Feint attacks were previously made on the Lens and Lille fronts.

The assault took place at 3.50 a.m. on the 31st July. The first line, a thousand yards ahead, was gained with ease, and also the second another thousand yards on, except on the extreme right of the Fifth Army, from Westhoek southwards, where machine guns had escaped the bombardment. In spite of heavy rain setting in in the afternoon, the centre and left of the Fifth Army and the French reached the first objectives for the day without serious difficulty, and the Second Army gained a line abreast of the right of the Fifth.

Weather then rendered a general advance difficult, and there was only some local fighting in which, on the 10th August, the position near Westhoek was improved.

Rain having ceased and the ground beginning to dry, it was decided to resume operations on the 16th August, and on the 15th two Canadian divisions made a diversion attack at Lens. Unfortunately, there was a heavy fall of rain on the night of the 15th/16th; however the whole of the objectives on the left, including the village of Langemarck from a point over 2,000 yards east of that village to the French left were won, but again on the right the gain of ground was slight.

Minor attacks to improve the line were made on the 22nd

46

(by the three right corps of the Fifth Army) and the 27th, but very heavy rain set in again on the 27th, and operations were again stopped.

As the delays had enabled the enemy to concentrate his forces and bring up reserves. Sir D. Haig decided to wait and prepare another formal offensive, and he extended his front of attack on the right to include another 3,000 yards. The main share in the attack was now allotted to the Second Army, which took over the right corps sector of the Fifth, where the Australian Corps had replaced the II.

The second offensive (Battle of the Menin Road) by the Second and Fifth Armies took place on 20th September.

The ground had dried up considerably since the previous operations, but unfortunately rain fell heavily during the night 19th/20th September, which was followed by thick mist in the morning. The Second Army employed three Corps, IX, X and I Anzac. The Fifth Army two and a half corps.

Only a short advance of some thousand yards was set down for this day for the Second Army and all objectives were taken although the enemy put up a stubborn defence in the neighbourhood of the Tower Hamlets.

We captured 44 officers and 1,564 other ranks by 6 p.m. 21st September in the Second Army. After the above attack the situation remained unchanged till the morning of 25th September. That day is one which I remember well. With our plans all complete for our offensive to take place early on 26th September, it was very disconcerting to be attacked ourselves on the 25th and it appeared at one time as if our plan for the 26th would not materialise.

At 6 a.m. on the 25th September, the enemy attacked in force our positions between Tower Hamlets and the Polygon Wood. The attacking troops penetrated our front and support lines in the Veldhoek trench north of the Menin Road, and for 500 yards south of the Polygon Wood. The support lines of the Veldhoek trench were re-captured by the Queens and Highland Light Infantry.

About 12 noon, a second heavy attack developed on the same front, which succeeded in driving in our line again in several places. The situation was, however, restored later during the afternoon by an attack carried out by troops of the Queens, Highland Light Infantry, Worcesters, Kings, Middlesex, Argyle and Sutherland Highlanders, and Australians.

The 33rd Division, however, suffered heavy casualties during the fighting on the 25th September, which not only reduced their fighting strength for the attack next morning, but also interfered considerably with the preparations for attack.

During the night 25th/26th September, the situation quietened down, which enabled our attacking troops to move forward to their assembly formations.

At 5.50 a.m., on the 26th September, the attack was launched on a frontage of 5,500 yards extending from the Bitter Wood opposite the southern extremity of the Tower Hamlets Spur to 500 yards north of Anzac. The Fifth Army continued the attack to the north. The X Corps on the right attacked with troops of the 39th Division. The I Anzac Corps attacked with the 5th and 4th Australian Divisions with complete success. The 4th Australian Division crossed the Upper Steenbeck Valley and gained both their objective lines south of Zonnebeke.

All day on the 26th our aeroplanes were very active; contact patrols flew low over the enemy's positions from early morning onwards, searching for reserve troops, and harassing hostile troops and transport from an average height of about 300 feet. A considerable amount of artillery cooperation was carried out and several special reconnaissances made. Several tons of bombs had been dropped daily and nightly during recent operations on enemy dumps, railheads, assembly areas, and traffic routes. Hostile aircraft were very active on the 26th, both trying to hinder our own machines and also flying low over our lines. Five of these low-flying aeroplanes were shot down by our machine-gun fire. In air fighting on 26th three E.A. were shot down and two driven down out of control; four of our machines were missing.

The number of prisoners passed through corps cages for the forty-eight hours up to 6 p.m., 27th, was 31 officers and 849 other ranks. The total since 6 p.m., 19th instant, was 79 officers and 2,466 other ranks.

The following is an extract from a memorandum which I issued after the above operations which shows the importance the enemy attached to ground and observation:

In yesterday's operations the enemy appears to have put forth extraordinary efforts to stop our advance or to drive us back from positions gained. As the detailed information continues to come in it is apparent that he recognised this attack, coming as it did so closely after that of the 20th, as the most critical one in our general advance toward the remaining positions on the Gheluvelt-Zionnebeke Ridge which he has so desperately defended.

The Battle of Menin Road on the 20th disclosed the importance the enemy attached to the Tower Hamlets Ridge. Yesterday's battle (Polygon Wood) not only brought about a renewal of counter-attacks on Tower Hamlets but developed fierce and sustained resistance south of Polygon Wood and very determined efforts to counter-attack on a large scale between it and Zonnebeke.

The very heavy counter-attack which the enemy launched at night against Tower Hamlets Ridge was to be expected after his extensive preparations throughout the day. These were disclosed by the movements in the localities and roads south-east of Zandvoorde and by the very heavy concentration of artillery behind Tenbrielen. This warning and the general anticipation of an attack on this sector—based on his previous action—enabled annihilating fire to be brought against his troops assembled and deploying and so disconcerted his attack that but few elements even got to close range. It is not to be expected that the enemy will abandon his efforts in this locality so long as he can deny us observation about Menin Road and Gheluvelt; his fears for Zandvoorde Ridge will continue to draw in a certain number of troops from the south, as has been the case in both operations.

The desperate manner in which he has fought to retain the advantage he gained about the Reutelbeek, south of Polygon Wood, on the 25th, indicates the importance the enemy attaches to observation from the heads of the valley between Gheluvelt and Becelaere. The circumstances of his attack on our line here the day before our own attack (described above in this summary) indicate how much he was willing to pay for denying us this ground.

There are indications that at least two of the divisions in the line, *viz.* 3rd Reserve Division and 50th Reserve Division, have had severe casualties and may be expected to be immediately relieved—the former has very low morale, having had numerous desertions, while one platoon surrendered in a body and a company refused to go forward. Of the reserve divisions, it may be considered that parts of two, the 17th and the one counter-attacking at Tower Hamlets, have had very severe losses, probably aggregating another division.

The 28th and 29th September passed relatively quietly. An interesting incident occurred on the 28th on the front of the 5th Australian Division, east of Polygon Wood, which well showed the demoralising effect of our tactics. A hostile party of some 200 of the 19th Reserve Division came into the line on the night of the 27th/28th. They were caught by our nightly artillery harassing fire, and then lost their way. Daylight found them wandering about close to the Australians, who opened on them with rifle and machine-gun fire. They suffered many casualties, and three officers and 67 other ranks surrendered in batches during the course of the morning.

The long spell of fine weather broke on the evening of the 3rd October, when a heavy gale accompanied by light rain showers, broke in from the south-west. There was some intermittent hostile shell fire during the night of 3rd/4th, but on the whole the assembling of our troops was not seriously interfered with.

At 6 a.m., 4th October, the attack was launched on a frontage of about 9,700 yards, extending from Bitter Wood, south of the Tower Hamlets Spur, to north of Gravenstafel, where the front of the attack was prolonged by the army on our left by a further 4,300 yards to the Ypres-Thourout Railway.

The IX Corps attacked on the right and the X Corps attacked on the right centre. Despite some hostile shelling of the forward area, the troops reached their assembly positions up to time. Considerable opposition was met with about Polderhoek Château and west of Reutel, but the objective was gained throughout the whole line, and the troops detailed for the assault on the further objective were able to reach their jumping-off positions up to time.

The I Anzac Corps attacked in the left centre with troops of the 1st and 2nd Australian Divisions. The enemy were met with in considerable strength, elements of three divisions being found formed up ready for an attack on our line which our assault anticipated only by ten minutes. Very severe casualties were inflicted on the enemy by our barrage and with the bayonet, and the enemy's opposition was quickly overcome. By 8.12 a.m. the whole of the Red Line was reported to be in our hands.

The II Anzac Corps attacked on the left with the 3rd Australian Division on the right and the New Zealand Division on the left. The New Zealand Division was intermittently shelled throughout the night, causing some casualties. The support line of the 3rd Australian Division was also intermittently shelled and at 5-30 a.m., the enemy opened a barrage on our front line. Nevertheless, our assault was launched punctually to time and by 9.14 a.m. both divisions had reported the capture of the whole of the Red Line, and many German prisoners were already being sent back.

After a halt of from one to two hours on the Red Line, the assault was launched on the Blue Line.

The X Corps attacked on the right, the I Anzac Corps attacked in the centre, and the II Anzac Corps attacked on the left with Australian and New Zealand troops.

The enemy offered a stubborn resistance, but by 12.20 p.m. the I Anzac Corps reported the capture of the whole of their final objective and the II Anzac Corps reported similarly at 1.15 p.m. The 7th Division, X Corps, reached practically the whole of their final objective and probably the 21st Division also, but the situation of the right brigade of this division in Reutel was at all times somewhat obscure.

During the day the enemy delivered no less than ten counter-attacks.

Five counter-attacks were made against the right brigade of the 5th Division between the Menin Road and Polderhoek Château and two attacks against the left brigade of the 21st Division on the Judge Copse Spur north of Reutel. These attacks appear to have been successfully repulsed. A further attack, however, succeeded in dislodging us from Judge Copse, Reutel and Polderhoek Château, and at the end of the day our line ran along the western and northern edges of Polderhoek Château Wood, the eastern edge of Cameron Covert, on the western outskirts of Reutel, through J 11 central to the Broodseinde-Becelaere Road at point J 6 c 1.o.

Further north, a concentration of the enemy's infantry in D 30a during the afternoon was dispersed by our artillery.

At 2.35 p-m. the enemy made a determined attack in three waves from the direction of the Cemetery in D 17a, north of Ypres-Roulers Railway, but this attack was broken up by our artillery, rifle and machine-gun fire. A second attack was similarly dealt with, and a concentration in D 4b and D 5a, west of Passchendaele, about noon was broken up by our artillery before any counter-attack from this direction could materialise. Several S.O.S. signals were sent up at various points of the front at 7 p.m. and during the night of 4th/5th October, but the enemy made no further attacks and the consolidation of our line proceeded satisfactorily.

On the greater part of our front the enemy offered a stubborn resistance and the large proportion of bayonet wounds among the German prisoners testifies to the severity of the hand-to-hand conflict which took place on many parts of the front, and in which our troops again proved their superiority. In places, however, the Germans surrendered freely, an Australian officer capturing 31 prisoners single-handed from one blockhouse, and the garrison of another blockhouse surrendered with three machine guns as soon as our attack was launched.

The enemy Order of Battle on the Second Army front of attack from north to south was as follows:

10th Ersatz Division, 20th Division, 4th Guard Division, one regiment of 45th Reserve Division, one or more battalions of 16th Division, 19th Reserve Division, 8th Division.

As a result of recent operations, it is estimated that seven battalions of each of the 4th Guard and 19th Reserve Divisions; six battalions each of the 13th Ersatz and 20th Divisions; five battalions of the 45th Reserve Division; four battalions of the 8th Division and three battalions of the 16th Division have all suffered so heavily as to be of little further fighting value. The thickening up of the line by the bringing in of battalions and regiments of other divisions, the confusion of units and the lack of cohesion in the counter-attacks proves how completely our former attacks have disorganised the enemy and with what haste he has been compelled to throw in his reinforcements. The enemy situation has not been improved by the severe losses which he incurred on 4th October.

In spite of very unfavourable weather on the day of attack, our aeroplanes succeeded in carrying out several contact patrols and flash reconnaissances and in attacking enemy troops and transport with machine-gun fire. One enemy aircraft was brought down by Lewis-gun fire on the I Anzac Corps front.

Seven field guns, several trench mortars and a large number of machine-guns have been captured.

The total number of prisoners who passed through Corps Cages and Casualty Clearing Stations from 6 p.m., 3rd October, to 6 p.m., 6th October, was 114 officers and 4,044 other ranks.

A study of the map will show my readers the immense importance of the possession of the Broodseinde Ridge which brought us within 1½ miles of Passchendaele and the high ground to the north of it.

The front of attack by the Second and Fifth Armies (Second Army Corps, Fifth Army Corps) measured some 10,000 yards. An attack prepared under great difficulties and at short notice and carried out with complete success by those gallant British and Dominion troops.

Dr. Bean, the Australian official historian, puts it:

An overwhelming blow had been struck, and both sides knew it. The objective was the most important yet attacked by the Second and Fifth Armies, and they had again done almost exactly what they pleased to do. . . . This was the third blow struck at Ypres in fifteen days with complete success. It drove the Germans from one of the most important positions on the Western Front. Notwithstanding their full knowledge that it was coming, they were completely powerless to withstand it.

Another writer says; "Who has ever heard of Broodseinde? (Try it on your friends.)"

Is that quite fair either to the memory of the gallant men who lie below those little white crosses in that hallowed ground or to their relatives throughout our great Empire? I wonder.

The Battle of Broodseinde on 4th October appears to have inflicted such heavy losses on the enemy and to have so disorganised his artillery that the succeeding days passed uneventfully.

Amongst many valuable documents and maps captured during the Battle of Broodseinde there fell into our hands a brigade order of the 5th Guards Infantry Brigade, showing that the enemy realised that the policy of counter-attack which they had practised throughout the whole of the operations at Ypres this year have been not only fruitless but costly. It was not proposed to hold the front line in much greater strength, not less than half the regiment being in the front line. From subsequent events it was found that this order came from the higher command and was already being put into effect.

The assembling of our troops during the night 8th/9th October was attended with considerable difficulty. The ground was very heavy owing to heavy rain having fallen intermittently since the afternoon of the 4th October, and the night up till 11 p.m. was exceptionally dark. No interference, however, was encountered from hostile artillery fire, and at 5.23 a.m. on the 9th October our attack was successfully launched.

The X Corps undertook a subsidiary operation on the right to improve the line we had gained on the 4th instant. The I Anzac Corps formed the right flank of the main attack and employed troops of the 2nd Australian Division, troops of the Fifth Army attacking on their left.

The enemy's artillery shelled the front areas of our two northern corps somewhat heavily at intervals during the night 11th/12th October, using a large number of gas shells on the area astride the Ypres-Roulers Railway and on Westhoek Ridge. This, together with the muddy ground and very wet, dark night, made the assembling of our troops a matter of considerable difficulty. All our troops, however, reached their jumping-off positions up to time, and at 5.25 a.m., 12th October the I and II Anzac Corps, consisting entirely of Australian and New Zealand troops, advanced to the assault. Hostile machine-guns immediately opened heavy fire, and it was found that new apron wire had been erected round several of the enemy's strong points and "pill boxes."

Our troops progressed satisfactorily up several of the spurs, but a strong point about Bellevue succeeded in checking our advance at this spot. The valleys proved impassable after the heavy rain owing to the mud, which also delayed and tired out our troops in their further progress on the higher slopes. Eventually our advance was brought to a standstill, and a line was consolidated slightly in advance of that from which the attack started.

The above was part of an attack launched by all three armies, 2nd and 5th British and the French (General Anthoine) on a 13,500-yards front. In places the first objective was reached, but at the end of the day, though the left of the Fifth Army and the

French made good progress, the right of the front line rested between the old line and the first objective.

After the operations of the 12th October had ceased there was no further change in the situation until the morning of the 26th. Close touch was maintained with the enemy everywhere except on part of the front of the I Anzac Corps, where the Germans have evacuated some low-lying ground south of the Ypres-Roulers Railway.

Every effort was made to organise the captured battle ground for further offensive operations.

Our troops having been successfully assembled without serious interference by the enemy an attack was launched at 5.40 a.m. on the fronts of the X and Canadian Corps.

Very heavy fighting took place during which our troops succeeded in capturing Gheluvelt village and Polderhoek Spur but were unable to hold on to either owing to the enemy powerful counter-attacks.

The weather conditions and the state of the ground had a very great influence on the day's operations.

Two features, apart from exhaustion and the difficulties of movement, seem outstanding:

(1) The mud, in a semi-liquid state and splashed up by shell bursts, got into everything, and was especially troublesome for rifles and machine guns.

(2) The very soft nature of the ground apparently affected the detonation of percussion shells to such an extent that prisoners have on several occasions remarked on the harmlessness of the bursts, or the failure to detonate.

On the 27th October it was found that the enemy was holding Decline Copse. He was, however, successfully ejected on the night 27th/28th October and the wood remained in our hands.

On the 28th and 29th October there was no change in the situation. The enemy's artillery concentrated heavily on our forward system in reply to our preparatory barrages on the mornings of the 27th and 28th October. During the night 29th/30th October, the situation was comparatively quiet.

Until about 11 a.m. on the 30th October the weather was fine, but it was very cold and a high wind was blowing. The assembly of the Canadians was successfully completed before dawn.

At about 2.43 a.m. the 1st Australian Division established a post in Decoy Wood, in order to cover the right flank of the attack.

At 5.53 a.m. an attack was launched by the Canadian Corps against the slopes to the west and south-west of Passchendaele. This, in conjunction with an attack by the XVIII Corps of the Fifth Army on their left.

The Order of Battle right to left was: 1st Australian Division, 4th Canadian Division, 3rd Canadian Division, and the 63rd Division of the Fifth Army.

During the course of the day the 3rd Canadian Division was counter-attacked no less than five times from the north of Passchendaele. All these attacks were successfully repulsed.

Again, the factor which chiefly affected the situation during the battle was the condition of the ground.

Although at the time of the attack and for some hours after the weather was fair, the rain in the afternoon seriously interfered with consolidation and supply. While these conditions were doubtless of advantage to the enemy in his defence, they may have affected his operations in counter-attack, especially in the afternoon and evening.

In general, the enemy has appeared considerably disorganised in connection with this operation. There is no doubt that some of his troops ran away early in the morning in one sector north of Passchendaele and that only a vigorous counter-attack by fresh troops from support re-established conditions. This may be the origin of the enemy's extraordinary statements in his wireless *communiqué* on the evening of the 30th, in which he said that we had captured Passchendaele and that they had recaptured it in an "impetuous attack. . . ."

On the 6th November further attacks were made by the Canadian and X Corps by which a little further ground was gained.

There was no change in the situation on the 7th, 8th and 9th November. These three days passed comparatively quietly on the battle front and there was a noticeable decrease in hostile artillery activity south of Sanctuary Wood.

This was probably owing to the fact that the enemy was moving guns northwards to the Westroosebeke area.

At 6.5 a.m. on the morning of the 13th November an attack was launched north of Passchendaele by the II and Canadian Corps. The order of battle from right to left was as follows:

2nd Canadian Division.

1st Canadian Division.

1st Division.

Each division was on a one-brigade front.

The attack progressed favourably and all objectives were obtained at an early hour, comparatively slight opposition being encountered.

Thus, ended what may be called the Passchendaele operations with Passchendaele in our hands and a substantial footing on the Passchendaele-Staden Ridge. Critics will say and have said "Yes, and at what a price?

I cannot dispute that. Those stages up to Passchendaele have always been a nightmare to me as they were to my chief. They were all right up to and including Broodseinde, 4th October. After that Fate was very cruel to us. It is easy to say now that everyone knew it was going to rain like that except those at G.H.Q. and that the whole operation was an "unjustifiable gamble." I do not know how any operation of war can be anything else but a gamble unless the enemy tells you what he has got the other side of the hill and in what state his troops are.

According to the German official monograph, *Flandern* 1917, no less than eighty-six German divisions twenty-two of them twice, had been thrown into the battle. There had been no change in the German strength on the Western Front during August, but from the beginning of September onwards there was a constant flow of reinforcements from the Eastern to the Western theatre. To quote the monograph:

Divisions disappeared by dozens into the turmoil of the battle, only to emerge from the witches' cauldron after a short period thinned and exhausted, often reduced to a miserable remnant. . . . Significant signs of strain manifested themselves.

On the 11th October Crown Prince Rupprecht recorded in his diary:

Most perturbing is the fact that our troops are steadily deteriorating.

General von Kuhl, Crown Prince Rupprecht's Chief of the Staff, in his account of Passchendaele in his *Weltkrieg*, states that the field recruit depots were completely emptied, and that by the 1st November the average strength of battalions on the whole Western front was down to about 640 men:

Except for the Class 1899, 18-year old men, there were available to replace losses only recovered wounded and men who could be withdrawn from the Eastern front, so that finally the recruit situation decisively influenced the conduct of the war.

The above at any rate shows that he was not too happy. I was, at that time, too junior to know anything about Cabinet plans and the situation in other theatres of war. I never served, at G.H.Q. I had only one task and that was to help my chief to capture Passchendaele. I presume the commander-in-chief had to take into consideration the state of the French Army at the time, the Italian disaster at Caporetto, the forthcoming Cambrai operations, the state of affairs on the Russian front and all factors which made it imperative that the Germans should not be at liberty to remove troops from Flanders.

I am quite unaware whether Sir Douglas Haig after Broodseinde ever considered the abandonment of further operations. I certainly never heard either him or the army commanders ever mention such an idea.

I venture to think that if we had not been "killed by mud" we should have taken the Passchendaele-Staden Ridge with proper preparations and if we had done so there would have been no 21st March, 1918 disaster, and no 8th April attack on us in Flanders. With that high ground in our possession as a jumping-off place for the spring of 1918, I am convinced that the enemy would not have had troops to spare for many other theatres.

To Italy

Passchendaele was soon to have a sequel. It had been a terribly hard time for all. No words can ever express what those gallant troops had gone through in order to get it. Anyhow it was ours and the objective had been gained after very great losses. Our object then was to hold it and to try and improve the awful conditions behind the lines and to prepare for the winter.

How well I remember one evening when an *aide-de-camp*, Captain Butler came in to my room to tell me that the chief wished to see me at once.

I went up to his room where he was sitting with a telegram before him. He just looked up and said: "You and I have got the sack. We are to hand over to General Rawlinson at once."

I confess that I was staggered at what seemed a grave injustice to my chief. Then he added; "We are to go to Italy at once."

No doubt the telegram had been a great shock to him, so with his keen sense of humour he thought he would just play it off on me.

It is interesting to quote from letters from my chief to his wife at this period. On 31st October he writes:

I have not read Lloyd George's speech and shall not now. I should not worry about that. It really does not matter in the least.

On 6th November he writes:

I sent you a wire this afternoon to say we had a good day. It was only a small one as we had not many troops engaged but we got Passchendaele which we have been working up to for some time and that in itself is a good thing.

On 7th November he writes:

I have just received a great shock. I have been ordered to go to Italy to assume command of the British Force there. I am very sick about it and do not want to go in the least.

The next day he writes:

The more I think of it (the command in Italy) I am afraid the less I like it. We leave for Paris on Saturday morning and go off to Italy on Sunday. I simply loathe leaving the Second Army and feel very depressed.

On the 9th he writes:

I have had rather a trying day, mostly saying goodbye. I saw the Canadian divisional generals and Currie early this morning and then went on to G.H.Q. where I saw D. H. I must say he was very nice. No one could have been nicer. He recommended one of the others to go.

The above hardly agrees with the statement which appeared recently that he was so glad to get away from Flanders.

The next few days were spent in handing over and in preparing a staff for Italy.

Incidentally, we had both hopes to get a few days' leave after Passchendaele had been captured.

Our journey to Italy was eventful. On the way a message arrived saying that Mr. Lloyd George wished to see the chief at the Hôtel Meurice in Paris.

I attended that meeting. Sir Maurice Hankey was also present. Monsieur Painlevé attended. Mr. Lloyd George was very insistent on the necessity of restoring the Italian Front and was only too anxious to take as many troops from the Western Front as my chief could wish.

We then went on to Padua, where the chief took over command from Lord Cavan, and we met Sir Henry Wilson, Marshal Foch, General Weygand and General Diaz, the Italian commander-in-chief.

I remember an amusing incident *en route*. We stopped at some station—I think Mantua—where we had arranged to have dinner in the station restaurant. As our train pulled up, we saw the station was all decorated with flags and the platform absolutely packed with people. We thought it was in honour of our chief who hurriedly got ready to receive a deputation of welcome. As nothing happened, we found on inquiry that this immense demonstration was to honour the first Italian soldiers who were returning to the Front after being wounded and that it had nothing whatever to do with us. We, with difficulty, made our way through the crowd to the restaurant.

We detrained at Padua.

Lord Cavan and his staff, which included the Prince of Wales and General Gathorne Hardy, were there, but, I think, only one battalion of the 23rd Division had arrived. Five divisions were *en route*.

Padua was in a state of turmoil. The streets were full. All the servants had fled from the principal hotel. The Second Italian Army was in retreat from Caporetto. We passed thousands of them marching back in quite an orderly manner.

During this time, we had many conferences with General Diaz and his Chief of Staff—General Guardino—and we learnt a good deal of the situation from our military *attaché*, General Delmé Radcliffe. We also had several conferences with Marshal Foch and General Weygand, and Sir Henry Wilson.

As far as I can recollect, it was decided that the Italian troops were to stand on a certain line and that the British troops should be put in to strengthen it.

I remember carrying out a reconnaissance in a Lancia car which had been lent to us previous to the arrival of our own cars. The Italian driver was certainly the most dangerous I have ever known. I recollect, very vividly, coming down the side of a precipice with the car apparently out of control. I could see one small heap of stones and mercifully the car hit them and this steadied us. I was unable to talk Italian to the driver but I think he was able to understand something of the language which I did use.

All seemed so peaceful after the Ypres Salient. The British troops were put into the Montello Sector. It was possible to ride and in some cases motor into the front line—a pleasant change from Flanders. As a matter of fact, although peaceful in the front line, it turned out to be far from peaceful in the rear. The French and British Headquarters had been established in Padua and we were very comfortable until the Austrian Air Force discovered our whereabouts. We had no air defences and we were at the mercy of the enemy bombers who followed the line of the canal, and gave us a bad time. The houses had no cellars and it was impossible to get any cover. The enemy bombers came over every half-hour.

We were eventually forced to move our headquarters to a place some six miles outside Padua, but not before an unfortunate incident had occurred. We had a large mess for the members of the Army Headquarter Mess quite close to our offices. One night I had a terribly heavy cold and the army commander flatly refused to allow me to go back to my office after dinner, as I always did. That very evening about 9.30 p.m. a heavy attack was made. Several bombs just missed the army mess, one killed a sentry on our headquarters and wounded a clerk of mine. All my office was destroyed. Such is fate. In an earlier chapter I described how my divisional commander, having a cold, sent me to the Canadian Corps as brigadier-general, general staff instead of to the 12th Corps in Salonika and in this instance a cold of my own saved me.

There is little to relate of our time in Italy except to say that we established the most friendly relations with General Diaz and his staff and with the Duke D'Aosta and other corps commanders.

A certain number of letters have appeared in the Press from time to time detracting from the services of the Italian troops and representing that the retreat from Caporetto was only stopped by the French and British troops almost at the point of the bayonet. That is totally untrue and I am fortunate in having in my possession a copy of a report rendered by General Sir Herbert

Plumer in March, 1918, just before handing over to Lord Cavan on our return to Flanders.

In this General Plumer states that the instructions which he received on proceeding to Italy were:

(*a*) To take command of the British Force then in transit to Italy;

(*b*) to report on the general situation and the number of troops required for the task before us.

He found on arrival that the general situation was certainly disquieting. The Italian Army had just received a very severe blow from which it was bound to require time to recover and reorganise, and although every effort was being made to dispatch the French and British forces to the theatre of operations, it was obvious, owing to the limited railway facilities, that some time must elapse before these forces could be regarded as a material factor.

Reconnaissances were made at once to arrange for their employment according to the number available and the development of the situation.

The Italian retreat had been arrested on the River Piave, but it was uncertain whether they would hold this line and in the first instance it was arranged that in conjunction with the French two of our divisions should move forward on arrival to the hills north and south of Vicenza, where a stand could certainly have been made.

The forward march was well carried out. The marches were necessarily long as time was, or might have been, all important. The troops everywhere met with an enthusiastic reception from the inhabitants.

By the time we had reached the above position the general situation had improved and we accordingly made an offer in conjunction with the French to take over sectors in the foothills of the Asiago plateau, which would have placed us in a strategically sound position to withstand attack either from the north or north-east. At this stage, however, snow was imminent and it was considered by the Italian High Command that our troops would suffer considerable losses and hardships from the cold in the hills, especially as they were unaccustomed to such warfare and there were many difficulties in providing the special mountain equipment necessary, and it was suggested that we should instead take over the Montello Sector with the French on our left, to which we agreed.

The Montello Sector was a feature by itself and an important one. It acted as a hinge to the whole Italian line, joining as it did that portion facing north from Mount Tomba to Lake Garda with the defensive line of the River Piave covering Venice, which was held by the Third Italian Army.

There is no doubt but that the entry of French and British troops into the line at this time had an excellent moral effect and it enabled the Italians to withdraw troops to train and reorganise.

There were at this time several German divisions east of the River Piave and it was quite likely that an attack to force the river and capture Venice was in contemplation. We took over the line on 4th December and at once got to work to organise the defences in depth, keeping as large a reserve ss was possible in hand, in case of unforeseen eventualities occurring in other portions of the line. Such did occur as the enemy commenced to develop local attacks on the Grappa and Asiago Sectors, first in one and then in the other, assisted undoubtedly by German batteries. These attacks fell principally on the first and fourth Italian Armies, who fought well and though they had a good number of casualties themselves they inflicted heavy losses on the enemy.

December was an anxious month. Local attacks grew more frequent and more severe and, though the progress made was not great and Italian counter-attacks were constantly made, yet the danger of a break through into the plains undoubtedly increased.

The general impression conveyed by these attacks was that the Austrians were being encouraged to persevere with their attacks in the hope of getting down into the plains for the winter and that the German divisions were being kept in Reserve with the intention of concentrating them at short notice to force home an attack should opportunity offer.

As a precautionary measure to meet this possibility it was arranged to form two groups, one to the east and one to the west of the River Brenta, each group composed of British, French and Italian troops. The object of these groups was not only to stop any enemy advance into the plains but to drive him back disorganised into the mountains where his losses would undoubtedly have been very severe.

Rear lines of defence were constructed under our supervision and as time passed and preparations became more forward the general atmosphere of security improved. This was increased by the attempt of the Italians to recapture Mount Asolone on 22nd December which resulted in the southern slopes being again in Italian hands. The following day, however, the pendulum again swung to the Asiago as the enemy captured Mount Melago and Col Rosso. The Italians re-took the former by counter-attack. Christmas Day found us, therefore, with the situation both on the Grappa and Asiago serious, the latter the more so, but the Italians, though suffering from prolonged strain and cold, were offering a stubborn resistance.

From this time the situation gradually improved. The French carried out a brilliant attack on 30th December in the Mount Tomba Sector, resulting in the capture of over 1,500 Austrian prisoners. British artillery assisted in this operation.

During all this period we had carried out continuous patrol work across the River Piave and much successful counter-battery work. The Piave was a very serious obstacle especially at that season of the year, the breadth opposite the British front being considerably over 1,000 yards and the current 14 knots. Every form of raft and boat had been used, but wading had proved the most successful, though the icy cold water made the difficulties even greater. In spite of this there was never any lack of volunteers both officers and men for these enterprises.

On 1st January our biggest raid was carried out by the Middlesex Regiment belonging to 41st Division. This was a most difficult and well-planned operation, which had for its objective the capture and surrounding of several buildings held by the enemy to a depth of 2,000 yards inland, provided a surprise could be effected. Two hundred and fifty men were passed across by wading and some prisoners were captured, but unfortunately the alarm was given by a party of fifty of the enemy that was encountered in an advanced post and the progress inland had, therefore, in accordance with orders, to be curtailed. The recrossing of the river was successfully effected and our casualties were very few. An operation of this nature requires much forethought and arranging, even to wrapping every man in hot blankets immediately on emerging from the icy water.

The Third Italian Army also opened the year well by clearing the Austrians from the west bank of the Piave about Zenson. This was followed on 14th January by the attack of the Fourth Italian Army on Mount Asolone which, although not entirely successful, resulted in capturing over 400 Austrian prisoners.

The situation had by this time so far improved that it was no longer necessary to keep the two precautionary groups, referred to above, in being, and Lord Plumer offered to take over another sector of defence on his right in order to assist the Italians. This was agreed to and was completed by 28th January. On this day and the following the First Italian Army carried out successful operations on the Col del Rosso-Mount Val Bella front on the Asiago plateau. The infantry attacked with great spirit and captured some 2,500 Austrian prisoners. British artillery took part in the above operation.

After the beginning of February, the weather became bad, a considerable amount of snow fell, and visibility was poor, which interfered considerably with air and artillery work.

It was certainly the case that the general situation on the Italian front had gradually but steadily improved during the four months which had elapsed since the British force was sent there and although we had not taken part in any serious fighting, I think we can fairly claim to have had some share in this improvement.

The work of the R.F.C. under Wing-Commander Webb-

Bowen during the period under review was quite brilliant. From the moment of arrival, they made their presence felt and very soon overcame the difficulties of the mountains. They took part in all operations and rendered much assistance to the Italians in the air. They carried out a large number of successful raids on enemy aerodromes, railway junctions, etc., and during the period destroyed sixty-four hostile machines, a large proportion of which were German, and nine balloons, our losses to the enemy during the period being twelve machines and three balloons, a record which speaks for itself.

The artillery also rendered very useful service. Our gunners soon became accustomed to the altered conditions and carried out many successful destructive shoots. A comparison of the photographs of hostile battery positions when our artillery entered the line with the positions now occupied shows that the enemy batteries had been successfully forced back almost throughout the whole front. Some British artillery assisted both in French and Italian operations and a frequent interchange of British and Italian batteries was made, together with Counter-Battery staff officers in order that experience of each other's methods might be gained. Every effort was made to illustrate the value of counter-battery work, the value of which we had learned by experience in France but which the Italians had not hitherto fully appreciated.

The Italians were only too anxious to profit by any experience we could give them and this was done not only by frequent interchange of visits of commanders and staffs to the various sectors of defence but by the establishment of Schools of Instruction at which a large number of Italian officers actually underwent the courses. About 100 Italian officers attended the courses at the various schools, together with some French officers. Similarly, British officers underwent courses at French and Italian schools.

The health of the troops had been very good and the casualties slight. The men felt the cold considerably during the winter, but Lord Plumer was convinced that they had benefited much from the change after the severe fighting they had had in France.

The conduct of the troops was excellent. They were very well received everywhere and they themselves set the high standard expected of them.

General Plumer stated in his report that he could not speak too highly of the kindness we received from the Italian authorities, with whom we established most cordial relations. Everything possible was done to help us. The provision, employment and maintenance of the Force entailed a considerable amount of work between the Allied Staffs and this was conducted throughout in complete harmony.

All the above is taken from an official dispatch rendered by General Plumer on leaving Italy.

During our time in Italy, Lady Plumer came out and they spent a happy ten days at Lady Carnarvon's villa at Porto Fino.

During this time, they visited all the hospitals at Genoa and in the neighbourhood. He received orders to return to the Western Front to resume command of the Second Army. After ten or eleven wonderful days they went by train to Rome for him to see the Italian Secretary of State for War and the ambassador, Sir Rennell Rodd, with whom they dined on the night of their arrival, and who arranged for them to see Queen Elena at the Quirinal and the queen-mother at her beautiful palace. He then returned to his headquarters to hand over his command to Lord Cavan and to bid farewell to a great many people. Some of his staff were on leave so they joined him on the Western Front. He and I travelled in a most comfortable coach provided by the Italian Government and met his wife at Turin, where she had just arrived from Rome.

RETURN TO THE YPRES SALIENT

Early in March, 1918, however, we were ordered back to Flanders—to our old headquarters at Cassel and we were quite glad to go back to our old haunts.

I may say that it was during our four months in Italy that the offer of Chief of the Imperial General Staff on certain well-defined conditions was made to Sir Herbert Plumer by Lord Derby. He was to replace Sir William Robertson, who was then Chief of the Imperial General Staff. It was at the time when the committee at Versailles under the late Lord Rawlinson was in existence and with which Sir William Robertson was never in agreement.

The conditions to be imposed on Sir Herbert Plumer did not give him a free hand over this committee and he would not accept the appointment on such conditions. Sir Henry Wilson was appointed shortly afterwards.

We returned to Cassel on 13th March, 1918, the army commander's birthday, and on the 21st March the storm broke on the Third and Fifth Armies. The reaction of which fell on the Second Army in April, as I will show later.

Shortly after our return to Cassel, the army commander received the following letter from the commander-in-chief showing how glad the latter was to have him back.

General Headquarters,
British Armies in France.
18th March, 1918.

My Dear Plumer,

I am giving this note to Cox, (now head of the Intelligence Branch), to introduce him to you. He is very level-headed and full of sense, so I hope you will have a good talk with him regarding the general situation of the enemy on this front.

I hope you are getting settled comfortably at Cassel. It is a great satisfaction to me to have you again at the head of an army here. I shall come and see you someday soon, meantime

Believe me,
Yours very truly,
D. Haig.

It is outside the scope of this book to go into the detail of the fighting with which the Second Army was not concerned, except to relate an incident at which I was present and which is engraved on my memory for ever.

On the afternoon of that fateful day, 21st March, 1918, my chief was sent for by the commander-in-chief, and I accompanied him. We were shown into Sir Douglas Haig's study where he was seated at a table. He seemed quite unmoved and after greeting us warmly he took us over to a big map in his room and explained to us the latest situation. It was unpleasant hearing. The enemy had broken through in many places and were heading for Amiens.

How well I remember the commander-in-chief's words, "What can you do to help?"

I may mention that we then had fourteen divisions in the Second Army, all in good condition. This was the number we had taken over on our return from Italy the previous week. We still held Passchendaele. The Messines-Wytschaete Ridge was held by three Australian divisions.

I am the only living witness of this scene.

The older man (Plumer) with his hand on the younger man's (Haig's) shoulder just ready to give the maximum and more to help his chief. His answer, "I will give you twelve divisions in return for tired ones."

To me it appeared impossible.

The commander-in-chief was obviously moved by it and said, "That means giving up Passchendaele."

"Not a bit of it," replied my chief without a moment's hesitation.

I can see the look of gratitude in Sir Douglas Haig's eyes as he saw us off in the car to return to Cassel.

The next few days were busy ones in sending those twelve divisions down south and receiving very tired divisions in their place.

Within a few days the Messines-Wyschaete Ridge was held by three weak brigades in place of three fresh Australian divisions.

With the help of the reinforcements which were hurried

both by the French and British, to the rescue, the situation in the south was stabilised.

It was during those days that the famous Doullens Conference was held.

Lord Milner and Sir Henry Wilson arrived and all the French officials. The army commanders and staffs were received and after a preliminary conference the army commanders and staffs were sent to sit in an adjoining room.

We sat and waited for hours.

I remember a wise remark of my old chief during those hours. "Byng and Gough ought to be with their armies instead of sitting here wasting time. It doesn't matter for you and me, as we are not engaged."

It was during those hours that Marshal Foch was made *generalissimo* and it was agreed that whatever happened the British would stand at Bray, at which place the French and British flanks would be joined.

By the time Byng rejoined his army after those wasted hours, the situation had changed and the British division holding Bray had already retired.

The situation again became difficult.

The commander of that division was removed. I think he had bad luck in being made a scapegoat.

Anyhow, the enemy was held up before Amiens and never again advanced in that theatre.

Early in April we had information of a possible enemy attack in the north. It was not thought that a major attack was contemplated but one that the enemy hoped would prevent further reinforcements being sent south.

Little did I imagine what was before me in the last month of my tenure as M.G.G.S. of the Second Army. I had just been appointed Deputy Chief of the Imperial General Staff to Sir Henry Wilson, but in view of the situation which developed I was allowed to remain with my chief till the 8th May.

The following is a summary of that eventful month:

1. On the 8th April it had been decided that the Second

Army should take over the front of the XV Corps as far south as the vicinity of Laventie in order to assist the First Army, which had extended its front to the south. It had also been agreed that the 50th Division in XI Corps should relieve the Portuguese troops which had been in the line for some considerable time.

The enemy, however, anticipated this movement and attacked the XI and XV Corps on the morning of 9th April, making considerable progress.

The taking over of XV Corps front by the Second Army was consequently postponed.

2. The situation of the Second Army at this time was as follows:

During the fighting on Third and Fifth Army fronts, which commenced on 21st March, it had been necessary to draw on Second Army for fresh troops, and of the 14 divisions in the Second Army on 21st March, all had been transferred to the south, with the exception of 29th and 49th, which were both under orders to go.

These divisions had been replaced by others from the south, which had all been heavily engaged and had since been filled up with reinforcements, and officers and N.C.O.'s who had only lately arrived in this country.

There had, however, been no indications whatever of attack on the Second Army front and the whole front, including the Passchendaele salient, was held intact.

3. As the attack on XI and XV Corps fronts on 9th April grew more serious, assistance was sent to XV Corps as under:

Two brigades of 29th Division to Merville area by bus.

One brigade of 25th Division to Steenwerck by road.

One brigade of 49th Division to La Crèche by bus.

4. The enemy succeeded in crossing the River Lys at Bac St. Maur and Sailly and by spreading north and south was soon able to increase the advantage gained, which seriously threatened Erquinghem and Armentières.

It was hoped that the brigade of 25th Division which arrived at Croix du Bac about 6 p.m. would be able to drive back any of the enemy that had crossed at Bac St. Maur, but they were unable to do this before dark.

5. On the following morning, 10th April, the attack spread to the right of the Second Army and after a heavy bombardment of the 19th and 25th Division fronts of IX Corps, the enemy succeeded in breaking through our line and advanced troops reached Messines about 8.30 a.m.

Counter-attacks were delivered at once, which regained the western edge.

Meanwhile the enemy made progress towards Ploegsteert village.

All available reserves were moved to reinforce IX Corps, *viz.*:

One brigade of 49th Division to Neuve Eglise.

One brigade of 29th Division to west of Ravelsberg.

One brigade of 36th Division to north-west of Neuve Eglise.

Instructions were received from G.H.Q. that 33rd Division would arrive from Fourth Army on night 10th/11th April, and 1st Australian Division would join XV Corps on 12th April.

6. The attack became general, and by the afternoon of 13th April it was evident that the enemy held Messines and that a gap existed between Messines and Wytschaete and between Ploegsteert and the Nieppe-Armentières Road.

It was also evident that the enemy had made considerable progress towards Steenwerck and that he was also attacking the Damstrasse.

Severe fighting was also going on in Estaires.

7. During the night 10th/11th April, the 9th Division established a firm hold on Wytschaete and the gaps mentioned above were filled by IX Corps.

About noon on 11th April the enemy began to threaten Neuve Eglise. We were at this time still holding Hill 63, and at 4 p.m. a heavy attack was launched against 19th Division about Messines.

The 9th Division reported that the attack at Hollebeke had

been repulsed.

By this time the 25th and 34th Divisions had had to withdraw from Le Bizet towards Nieppe, the enemy having pressed his attack north of Steenwerck.

Estaires had also fallen.

8. In order to economise troops, consequent on the above, it became necessary to withdraw the IX Corps on night 11th/12th April to the general line Steenwerck Station-Pont d'Achelles-Neuve Eglise-Wulverghem-Wytschaete, and to withdraw XXII, VIII and II Corps to their "battle zones," leaving outposts in advance.

This was accomplished successfully.

9. On 12th April the enemy pressed his attack against XV Corps, breaking through at Nerville and west of that place, and driving back 29th and 31st Divisions between Neuf Berquin and Merris.

This left a gap exposing Bailleul.

The XV Corps was taken over by Second Army at 12 noon on 12th April. The situation at this time was serious, as the 1st Australian Division was not due to begin detraining at Hazebrouck till the late afternoon.

By night the 33rd Division had filled the gaps and the 1st Australian Division was commencing to arrive to defend Strazeele, Borre and Pradelles.

10. 13th April was a heavy day, during which repeated attacks on 4th Guards Brigade and 33rd Division were repulsed before 4th Guards Brigade were forced back to the edge of Bois D'Aval.

Four attacks on 33rd Division south of Meteren were repulsed.

Attacks on Wulverghem were also repulsed and at 11 a.m. we lost Neuve Eglise, but regained it after heavy fighting.

11. During the night 13th/14th April, the 1st Australian Division relieved the 29th and 31st Divisions.

Repeated attacks were made on Neuve Eglise, which was

cleared by the Glasgow Highlanders of 33rd Division.

The 33rd Division south of Meteren was also attacked during the forenoon of 14th and held firm.

Several more attacks were made on the army front during the day, the most serious being against the 33rd Division south of Meteren where the enemy succeeded in penetrating outlines, but was successfully driven back by 1st Middlesex and New Zealand Entrenching Battalion.

By the evening of 14th two French Divisions (28th and 133rd) and three French cavalry divisions were concentrating on the general line Caestre-Poperinghe.

12. Except for heavy shelling on parts of the army front the 15th April was comparatively quiet up till 5 p.m., when the enemy launched a heavy attack by three divisions, including the Alpine Corps, and succeeded in capturing Bailleul and the Ravelsberg Ridge.

13. By 10 a.m. on 16th April the II Corps had withdrawn successfully to the Pilckem Ridge-White Château line and XXII Corps to Voormezeele line, with outposts in front.

Several enemy attacks were made on this day but were all repulsed.

The 28th and 133rd French Divisions were to have launched a counter-attack in conjunction with the British 9th Division at 6 p.m., but this did not materialize owing to there being insufficient time to get the troops into position.

14. On 17th April the 7th Seaforth Highlanders recaptured Wytschaete.

Other attacks made on the 19th, 33rd, 34th and 1st Australian Divisions were all repulsed.

On 18th April the Belgians completed the relief of 30th Division on the extreme north of the Second Army.

28th French Division took over responsibility for Kemmel Hill. On this date several attacks were made on 19th Division north of Kemmel, but were all repulsed.

15. During the next few days only local actions took place,

and during this time the 28th, 154th, 34th and 133rd French Divisions entered the line, the two former comprising the II French Cavalry Corps and the latter the XXXVI Corps, the command of the whole sector passing to General de Mitry from IX Corps.

This sector included the defences of Kemmel, Mont Rouge, Mont Moir, Mont Vidaigne and Mont des Cats.

The XV Corps, 1st Australian Division, also extended its front to north-east of Meteren.

16. On 25th April the enemy launched a heavy attack on the front Haegedoorne to The Bluff, after severe bombardment.

His intention was evidently to capture Kemmel from the south, combined with an attack from the east, south of Wytschaete.

During the morning the enemy made progress and captured Kemmel and Kemmel village, the line at 1 p.m. running west of Dranoutre along the Millekruisse-La Clytte road with elements apparently still on Kemmel Hill, the British being forced back north of Wytschaete.

Orders were at once given to secure the line from La Clytte to Hallebast and from Hallebast to Kruisstraathoek. Further reserves were moved up to Ouderdom, Dickebusch and Reninghelst, and 19th and 34th Divisions near Poperinghe were put under orders to move at short notice if required.

17. By the evening of 25th April the French line ran from north of Haegedoorne *via* Koudekot-Locre Château-Locre Hospice-south-east slopes of Sterrenberg-La Clytte. British line thence *via* Cheapside-Brasserie-Sniper's Barn-South of St. Eloi to The Bluff-Hill 60-Zillebeke-White Château and thence along Pilckem Ridge.

18. Orders were issued for the French D.A.N. to retake Kemmel and re-establish the line La Polka (inclusive)-Aircraft Farm-Donegal Farm-south of Dranoutre-Haegedoorne. The 25th British Division was placed under II French Cavalry Corps for the purpose of counter-attacking.

19. The attack was launched at 3 a.m. on 26th April by 39th French Division and 21st British Division.

The 21st Division penetrated through on a narrow front as far as the outskirts of Kemmel village, capturing fifty prisoners. The 39th French Division was held up on the line of the Kemmelbeek, the 21st British Division having subsequently to conform.

During the morning the enemy developed heavy attacks against the 9th British Division and captured the Spoilbank and the Brasserie after severe fighting, and after three unsuccessful attempts, captured Locre.

The 2nd Bedfords held on to The Bluff throughout the day.

20. Orders were given for the following readjustment of the line to be made on night 26th/27th April:

II Corps to hold the present line as outposts and to hold Canal Bank line as main line as far south as Menin Gate.

XXII Corps to hold from Menin Gate *via* Kruisstraathoek Line-Cheapside to junction with French on Kemmelbeek.

II Corps to man Brielen-Elverdinghe line and East Poperinghe line from 1,000 yards north-east of Peselhoek to Ypres-Poperinghe Road.

XXII Corps to man Kruisstraat-Cape Belge-Dickebusch-Millekruisse-La Clytte line.

French to hold line Fontaine Heuck-west of Croix de Poperinghe-Mont Rouge-Sterrenberg to La Clytte and defences of Mont Rouge-Mont Noir-Mont Vidaigne-Mont des Cats and East Poperinghe line from Reninghelst-Abeele Road *via* Piebruck Spur and west of Fontaine Heuck to junction with XV Corps north of Fletre-Meteren Road.

VIII Corps to hold with 34th and 59th Divisions the Brandhoek line from south of Ouderdom to Poperinghe-Ypres Road with posts in Vlamertinghe line, also East Poperinghe line from Ypres-Poperinghe Road to Reninghelst-Abeele Road.

Main Line.

Canal-Ypres Ramparts-Shrapnel Corner-Château Segard-Elzenwalle Ridge Wood-Cheapside.

Outpost Line.

Line of Steenbeek-Bossaert Farm-Wieltje-Potijze-White Château-West end of Zillebeke Lake-Lock 8-Voormezeele (this to be held as an advanced post, if possible).

This was successfully carried out as ordered, the Zillebeke Sluice Gates being destroyed.

21. On 27th and 28th April several local actions took place, principally at Voormezelle, the Mound and Locre.

22. On 29th April, after an intense bombardment which started at 3.10 a.m., the enemy attacked the fronts of 21st, 49th and 25th Divisions between 5 a.m. and 5.30 a.m., and was repulsed all along the line.

He attacked the 49th Division again at 6 a.m. and the attack was broken up, the enemy suffering severe losses in trying to advance in mass formation with bayonets fixed.

25th Division were attacked at 8.35 a.m.

During the morning the 25th Division repulsed four attacks; 49th Division repulsed repeated attacks and the brunt of the attack was borne by 2ist Division.

As the result, our line remained intact with the possible exception of a small sector of the advanced trench line.

23. The French were also heavily attacked about Locre.

Fighting continued throughout the day, especially in the region of Hyde Park Corner, which changed hands repeatedly.

It was thought that a serious attempt to capture Scherpenberg and Mont Rouge was in progress, but this at any rate was frustrated.

At the end of the day the French line ran through Locre Church, and Hyde Park Comer was in the hands of the French.

This was a very heavy day's fighting and the enemy losses were very severe.

24. The following divisions received special messages of congratulation from the Field-Marshal Commanding-in-Chief:

9th 21st 29th 33rd 49th
19th 25th 31st 34th 1st Australian.

There is no doubt that the 29th April was the critical day.

The enemy attack failed that day. In no sector did he gain ground of any importance. The failure of the attempt on the 29th April, which had very far objectives—a captured map showed one of the divisions engaged to have had an objective 3½ miles distant—appears to have convinced the enemy that nothing further was to be gained in Flanders without a complete reorganisation of his troops, which his position in a narrow salient made extremely difficult to hide.

We had certain indications that the enemy intended to make another attack between Locre and Zillebeke on the 4th May, but this never materialised.

He had shot his bolt in Flanders. We had just managed to stop him, but only just. I do not think that his original attack on the 9th April ever aimed at anything beyond a local success. I always think he launched his original attack against us at a very lucky moment, just as the 50th Division was relieving the Portuguese and that he obtained far more success than he anticipated. The local commander, having obtained this success, no doubt begged the permission of the high command to exploit it. It has happened many times before in history and no doubt will happen again. His gamble had failed, but only just.

We calculated that the enemy suffered some 120,000 casualties between the 9th April and the 8th August in the Lys Salient. 42 German divisions were employed in holding about 30 miles of line, a large portion of which was exposed to concentrated artillery fire, for over three months during the summer. The result was that the enemy found themselves exhausted in the north and with insufficient new troops to do anything in the south. Might not Sir Douglas Haig have found himself in the same position had he listened to the many attempts to get him to release troops from the Western Front? One knows how Sir William Robertson supported him in this. He was very averse to making detachments.

I maintain that the German advance from the 9th April, 1918, was a gamble which very nearly succeeded just as Gallipoli, was a gamble which very nearly succeeded. I have stood on, the point reached by Allanson and his gallant Gurkhas, and I have talked since with Turkish officers who were there and also in Constantinople at that time. It was just touch and go. One further effort, had it been possible, would have turned the scale and the Turks would have retired and a panic would have taken place in Constantinople. Had that taken place and the gamble succeeded no praise would have been too high for the brains which conceived it or for the troops which carried it out.

I often look back on that memorable month's fighting. On the visits which the army commander paid to those heroic divisions and brigades. To those units as they came out of the line for a well-earned rest. One must remember that they had nearly all been engaged only a month before in the German attack on the Third and Fifth Armies.

It was a gruelling month. We were literally hanging on by our eyelids.

A General Headquarters line far in the rear was being dug for us to retire to. How the chief hated the very mention of it.

What a tower of strength the late King of the Belgians was in those days. We saw him almost daily. He refused to entertain the idea of going back and he certainly did not want us to do so.

It was, indeed, a desperate situation.

We had hardly any reserves. Undoubtedly the enemy had gained a bigger success than he anticipated. He pressed home his advantage to the full and we lost our beloved Messines-Wytschaete Ridge, Kemmel and all our points of vantage for which we had fought so hard, but we still hung on to Passchendaele.

The enemy was almost astride our communications. He pressed right down to Meteren and beyond. It was obvious it could not go on. It was galling enough to have lost the Messines-Wytschaete Ridge—so well won in 1917—but here was our Passchendaele, for which so many lives had been given,

81

about to go.

I felt so much for our chief during those days.

One day, however, after consulting with the corps commander holding Passchendaele (Hunter Weston), I decided to suggest to the chief that we should have to withdraw from Passchendaele. I know how it stung him. "I won't have it," and he walked out of my room. A few moments afterwards he came back and laid his hand on my shoulder, saying, "You are right, issue the orders."

I wrote out those heartrending orders but, before they had gone, the chief came back to ask if they had gone.

He made another attempt to stop them.

It was a scene which I shall never forget. There was the man, who by sheer determination and pluck had held the Ypres Salient for years against all comers and who had gained Messines and Passchendaele, being forced to withdraw.

How he hated giving it up. He knew it had to be. He knew that it was necessary for the safety of his men.

I shall not forget the night our troops slipped out of Passchendaele and our front line was once again just in front of Ypres.

The weeks that followed were momentous ones. No words could adequately express the way in which the troops held on to their positions.

As stated above, nearly all the divisions had been fighting continuously since the 21st March. There were no fresh divisions.

The enemy launched attack after attack. A French Army Corps was sent up by lorry to our assistance and was put in the Kemmel Area.

We were bombed out of our Headquarters at Cassel and forced back to Blendecques, retaining Cassel as our advanced Headquarters.

The enemy broke through to Meteren and Strazeele.

How well I remember having to report to the chief that the army was in three pieces and his characteristic reply, "Well, that is better than being in four." Those words alone show his wonderful fighting spirit. It was, indeed, a near thing. The enemy at Strazeele—only a few miles from Hazebrouck and our line of communication.

We got word that the 1st Australian Division under Major-General Harold Walker was on its way to us by train. Could we hold on till then? We had no reserves. We turned out the students, servants and grooms from our Second Army School to hold on to Strazeele. Could we hold on?

Never shall I forget the message which said that the enemy had bombed Etaples Bridge and that the Australian Division would be four hours late.

Oh! those four hours.

I was at Hazebrouck when the trains at last arrived. I can see those Australian s detraining and advancing to Strazeele. Glorious fellows and so were the servants and grooms whom they had relieved.

It was a desperate and critical situation and I hope it will be dealt with fully in the *Official History of the War*.

Fortunately, the army as a whole did not know that we were in such desperate straits and literally down to our last man.

Through it all the nerve of the army commander who was bearing the responsibility never faltered. He knew, as I knew, how near it was. He endured those four hours. No one could, however, have foreseen that that was the end. The enemy effort was spent. He never attacked again. The Salient was saved. The Channel Ports were saved. The General Headquarters line which had been prepared in the rear was never required. Our chief had won through and that was all that mattered to us.

And so that month's fighting ended on 8th May, and with it my happy and close association with my dearly loved chief. I had to go off at once to take up my appointment as Deputy Chief of the Imperial General Staff, under the late Field-Marshal Sir Henry Wilson.

Although about to start another two and a half years of a very happy association with the *commandant* of the Staff College under whom I had served as a student, it meant nothing but long hours with difficult problems in the War Office. It was, however, a great experience which has since been of great help to me and I can never forget Sir Henry Wilson's goodness to me.

It was a great wrench to leave the Second Army—its great chief and the most wonderful and loyal staff. I treasure such wonderful letters from the chief on leaving. They are too sacred to publish. I may add that he felt things so much that he was always unable to say anything on such occasions as parting with a friend. Great tears used to roll down his cheeks but, nevertheless, his meaning was more than understood by his handshake.

During the time I have been writing this *memoir* I have heard from all the principal members of the old Second Army Staff. They all show the wonderful influence which he exercised over us all. How we all leapt with joy to meet his wishes. How we treasured the confidence which he placed in us. How well we all knew that, as long as we had done our best, our chief would back us through thick and thin whatever mistakes we might make. How by his own great personality he had made the way easy for us. It was he who had made corps, divisions, brigades and lower formations accept us everywhere as their friends and helpers.

We were accepted everywhere with open arms. He made it quite clear that staff officers are only servants of the troops. Any staff officer who had any idea that his red tabs gave him any authority to be superior came down with a very heavy bump. He had a glorious sense of humour. He loved to "pull our legs," especially mine. He loved an amusing story but would not for a moment tolerate any story over the border. He showed his displeasure in no uncertain way. He would not tolerate any familiarity in speech of any senior officers by junior ones. If anyone in conversation mentioned that "Rawly" or "Birdie," meaning Sir Henry Rawlinson or Sir William Birdwood, had done something, he would at once say, "I presume you mean Sir Henry Rawlinson or Sir William Birdwood." The offender did not do so again.

He was a very strict disciplinarian. No more fair or just man has ever lived, but he had a very high sense of duty and he spared no one who abused his goodness. A commander has many very unpleasant duties to perform both in war and peace, especially in the Great War where the strain and anxiety, loss of sleep, etc., told on so many until at length their places had to be taken by others. One knew well how hard they were fighting against being sent home. Many a time an officer has come into my office on the way to see the army commander full of protests, prepared to refuse at all costs to be sent home. The same officer has looked in again a few minutes after to say, "He was dead right," and went away bearing no malice. It is a gift to be able to do that. He had that gift.

Punctuality was another of his great qualities. Every morning he walked into breakfast at 7.30 a.m. Not one of us ever dared to be late, though we had some near shaves.

He hated a telephone and would never have one in his room. I remember so well when we went to Padua, I had a telephone in his room in the house which we occupied removed or rather hidden under a table. All of a sudden it went off under the table like an infernal machine. How he laughed. On that day another amusing incident occurred. The house was terribly cold and we only had wood fires which would not draw. One of his personal staff who could not speak a word of Italian was observed in a shop in Padua in British uniform on his knees blowing his cheeks out. He was apparently trying to buy some bellows and was successful.

Before I pass on to later times when I no longer had the honour of serving under him perhaps it would not be out of place if I tried to give a picture of him from the point of view of the staff officer who was privileged to serve him and to study his ways. I say at once that he was the supreme head, he listened to all and then made his decision, which was final. He liked to know exactly what was going on. He wished all matters of importance referred to him. He would not tolerate decisions, except on minor details, made without his knowledge. He kept his fingers on the pulse of everything. He kept all patronage in his own hands. Every appointment was approved by him personally. No one was ever appointed to the Second Army without being given every chance.

He had a wonderful way of making his wishes clear to his staff. He wrote very little himself but had an extraordinary faculty of putting his finger on where any draft submitted to him failed. I speak with great knowledge on this point as I can never remember an instance in which I did not readily admit that his alterations were a great improvement on my humble efforts. It was always interesting as we worked longer together to get nearer and nearer to his wishes. I can say with pride that before I left him, I often submitted memoranda which he approved without comment, which always pleased me.

His thoughtfulness for others was remarkable. How often did I find him in the office of the G.S.O.2. or G.S.0.3. or in the Intelligence Office ascertaining the latest information of the situation rather than have me disturbed if he thought I was busy, and the same with other senior officers of the staff.

In addition to his daily conferences by which he kept every branch of the staff in touch with the situation, he made a point of having a talk to each of the heads of his staff so that he knew and could help them with their difficulties.

GOODBYE TO FLANDERS, THE ADVANCE TO THE RHINE

There is little to relate from the Flanders front between May and September, 1918. All will remember that on the 8th August with the Fourth Army success in the south and the advance of the Australian and other troops, the German resistance began to crack. This reacted on the fronts of other armies and it may be said that in the early days of September, 1918, the general situation had become very favourable to the Allies. The hostile forces then opposed to the Belgian and the British Second Army were very weak, and the moment was ripe for offensive action on a large scale elsewhere by the British, French and American forces. The general plan was to carry out an operation with a view to clearing the Belgian coast and the country between that coast and the River Lys.

For this plan, the following troops were placed by Marshal Foch under the orders of His Majesty the King of the Belgians, in addition to his own: The British Second Army;

Three French infantry divisions, and one cavalry corps (three divisions).

The British Second Army, which comprised the II, XIX, X, and XV Corps, under command of General Sir H. Plumer, was, prior to the 28th September, 1918, holding the line from just north of Ypres to Armentières. The offensive on the British front was to be undertaken by II Corps, on right of the Belgian Army, and XIX Corps, on right of II Corps, on a front of some 4½ miles south of the Ypres–Zionnebeke road. The XV and X Corps, on right of the XIX Corps, were ordered to watch their opportunity and take every advantage of the enemy weakening on their front to press his retirement.

The attack was launched at dawn of 28th September, 1918, after an intensive artillery bombardment of three hours' duration. Field guns were placed at intervals of thirty-eight yards.

By the end of the day the British Divisions had passed beyond the farthest limits of the Third Battle of Ypres (July–November, 1917).

South of the main attack, the X and XV Corps had carried their line slightly forward.

The advantages gained were followed up with the greatest vigour, and by the morning of the 6th October the line Ledeghem–Comines–Warneton–Fresnelle had been reached.

The rapid advance of the British troops necessitated the re-establishing of adequate communications in the area of the old Ypres battles. Every effort was put forth, and by the 14th October the restoration of communications was sufficiently advanced to permit of a resumption of the offensive. (It was originally intended to resume the attack on the 7th October.) During the period 6th–14th October, in order to lead the enemy to suppose an immediate advance was imminent, and to stop the diversion of his troops to the Belgian front, intensive harassing fire was employed.

The advance of the Allied Armies in the direction of Valenciennes, which was threatening the German communications with the south, coupled with the advance of the troops under H.M. the King of the Belgians, which was seriously threatening Lille from the north, led to very obvious preparations being made for a retirement from Lille.

The enemy artillery became generally active on 13th October, and carried out a counter-preparation. The attack was launched at 5.35 a.m. from Comines northwards in conjunction with the Belgian Army on the left. The Order of Battle from north to south on the front of the attack was as follows:

II Corps (St. Pieter-Vijfwegen-Kazelberg Road);

XIX Corps (Vijfwegen-Kazelberg to 500 yards north of Gheluwe);

X Corps (500 yards north of Gheluwe to one mile west of Wervicq).

The attack was again attended with complete success. By 15.00 the general line on the Army Front ran: outskirts of Wervicq500 yards north of Wervicq-Menin railway-Coucou—1,000 yards west of Golleghaem-Steenbeek—1,000 yards east of Winkel St. Eloi. On this day enemy aircraft were active, and twenty of his machines were brought down. Three thousand, six hundred and seventy-three prisoners and 50 guns were captured during the day.

The advance was continued on 15th October and following days, and all objectives were taken and by 6 a.m. of 20th October the line Desselghem-Courtrai-Rolleghem-Leers was reached. By the 23rd October enemy resistance had considerably increased, there was much bombardment of back areas and gas shelling, he had evidently collected artillery for the defence of Lille, where also the entrenchments were most elaborate. A combined attack by the II and XIX Corps and the left division (34th) of the X Corps was therefore ordered for 25th October. A general advance of over 3,000 yards was made. Further advances were made on the 26th October, without, however, meeting with much opposition.

The advance was resumed at 5.25 a.m. on 31st October. The troops employed were XIX Corps (35th Division), II Corps (31st and 34th Divisions), attacking in conjunction with the French on the left, with the right flank on the Schelde, with objectives:

(1) Anzeghem-Bergstraat-Tieghem-Vierschaat.

(2) Belgie Cabt-Caster-Varent-Kerkhove.

All objectives were taken by 16.15 hours. On this day 1,125 prisoners were captured.

As the result of the attack, the Second Army completed the occupation of the left bank of the Scheldt on the whole front.

On the 1st November patrols of II Corps (34th Division) pushed forward and reached Boschkant, Gyselbrechten and Hill 83, without encountering any opposition, the enemy having apparently withdrawn owing to the success of the attacks on 31st October.

During the 3rd November posts were established east of the Scheldt near Herinnes and Tenhove. Hostile artillery was very active all the day on the Bessuyt-Avelghem front. Further crossings of the Scheldt were effected on the 4th November, the patrols crossing in boats. There was great air activity on this day, twenty enemy aircraft and four observation balloons being destroyed. On the 4th November at 12 noon the Second Army ceased to be under the command of H.M. the King of the Belgians and reverted to the command of the Field-Marshal Commanding-in-Chief.

Many villages were shelled with gas by the enemy on 6th November-8th November. During the night of 8th/9th November patrols succeeded in crossing the Scheldt at numerous points, encountering little resistance, and by 9 a.m. our troops were on the eastern bank of the river on the whole army front, crossing in boats and pontoons. The advance was more rapid on the southern portion of the army front. The XIX Corps established itself on the eastern bank of the Scheldt, and commenced its advance at noon of 9th November. The British Fifth Army (on the right) occupied Mount St. Aubert at an early hour, in touch with the 40th Division, XV Corps, (Second Army). At midday the following general line had been reached; Bourgogne-Clipet and along the Clipet-Anseroeul road to just south of Anseroeul-railway junction south of Orroir-Escanaffles—thence along the railway to east of Meersche, in touch with 41st French Division, which had passed one battalion over the River Scheldt south of Melden.

Progress was rapid throughout the day, and scarcely any resistance was encountered. By nightfall the XIX Corps had gained touch with the VII French Corps, which held Etrichove.

Orders were issued for the 31st, 35th and 41st Divisions (XIX Corps) to resume the advance at 9 a.m. on 10th November to the general line Hurdumont-Boschstraat-Rooverst-Haunstraat, in touch with the French on their left, and the X Corps on their right. These orders were carried out; practically no opposition was encountered, though the advanced troops were in constant touch with the enemy's rear-guards.

By nightfall the following line had been reached;

X Corps: Southern end of Bois de Leuze-Arbre St. Pierre-Ellezeiles, with patrols well in advance.

XIX Corps; Hurdmont—northwards to Hauwatraat, with advanced troops in Opbrakel and Nederbrakel.

On the following day, 11th November, the 29th and 30th Divisions (X Corps) and 31st, 35th and 41st Divisions (XIX Corps) advanced in the morning, and when hostilities ceased at n a.m., the 29th Division had reached the River Dendre front east of Hourain to north of Lessines (with a bridgehead east of Lessines), and the 30th Division was on a line east of Biercamp.

On the XIX Corps front, the 31st Division was just west of the Lessines-Grammont Road in touch with the 35th Division, which had reached the Dendre in Grammont, while the 41st Division was east of Gemeldorp, in touch with the 35th Division north of Grammont.

It was just before 11 a.m. on the 11th November that General Plumer heard that the Second Army had been chosen to be the Army of Occupation.

I think the most graphic way in which I can describe the advance to the Rhine is by giving extracts from the diary of Captain M. B. Heywood, D.S.O., M.V.O., of the Second Army Staff. This officer went out to the war as *A.D.C.* to General Plumer and did splendid work throughout the war on the Second Army Staff. His diary shows:

"*Nov. 13th.* We collected sixteen divisions that we were to take forward; 2nd, 3rd, 22nd and Canadian Corps, 4th Army on our right. The advance was very difficult as all bridges and roads were blown up, telegraph poles and trees fell across the roads, railway lines blown up about every 200 yards and we had to feed our troops by lorries making trips of 160 miles through the devastated area. Roads very narrow *pavé* with two or three feet of mud either side, all full of our prisoners, Italians, Portuguese and Alsatians and local inhabitants released by Germans. All very hungry, with no blankets. Our supplies came from Calais!

Nov. 17th, Sunday. Hard frost. Thanksgiving Service; 3,000 troops, (2,000 spectators) marched past in Grand Place Roubaix. General took salute from the old *kommandatur*, a satisfactory sight (Ruprecht of Bavaria's H.Q.).

Nov. 18th and 19th. Plans continually altered owing to different instructions from G.H.Q. Some of our troops had to come from parts of the line 60 miles away. All roads full of civilians absolutely dead beat. I always came back with my car full of women and babies.

Nov. 21st. Whole of our plan altered as only Second Army had to cross Frontier with the eleven divisions of 2nd, 4th, Canadian and 9th Corps. General re-shuffle.

Nov. 22nd. Attended march past of our troops in Brussels before the King and Sir Herbert.

Nov. 24th. Reached Namur after three punctures; one on the field of Waterloo.

Nov. 27th. Our first train reached Namur. Up to then lorries ran from Boulogne and Calais to Namur 250 miles, and the sleeper track over the Salient was almost impossible.

Nov. 28th. Our advance being held up owing to lack of food, motored to Spa to see Armistice commission. Disturbances in most of big towns as Belgians wrecking houses of people who had been friendly to Germans. Nice to be saluted by German sentries at Hôtel Britannique Spa; rear troops of Germans mutinous and undisciplined. By December 1st, supply situation very bad—General ordered two days halt. Our cavalry crossed frontier and halted 12 miles east of it.

Dec. 4th. Went with Phillip Hanson, V.C., to Bittsburg and watched our infantry across into Germany with fixed bayonets and bands playing—a glorious sight. Roads strewn with debris of German retreat; surprised at number of dead horses. German civilians took no notice of us. The whole time we had trouble with rations and in keeping divisions up to the march programme. The tail of the Canadian Corps was always lagging behind and 6th Corps bumping into them and so endless wrangling over billets. The men were very discontented as they had had no clean clothes or proper food since November 11th, and had marched a long way on bad roads. The civilian authorities in Germany were terrified of the revolution that was taking place and of the mutinous troops who were looting shops, and we had to get the Guards Division into Cologne before the programme date.

Dec. 10th. I went to Cologne and walked across the Hohenzollern Bridge, spending some time in looking at the Rhine about which we had talked so much during the last four years.

Dec. 12th. I stood with the army commander watching the cavalry cross the Rhine. As we arrived the Union Jack was broken from the mast-head just underneath the enormous equestrian statue of Kaiser William. The cavalry looked magnificent, and some Germans asked me why we had taken the trouble to rub the situation in by bringing picked troops out from England especially for the occasion. They crossed the Rhine to Tipperary, and the Soldiers' Chorus from *Faust*, and advanced to the neutral zone which was an arc of about 20 miles in diameter.

Dec. 13th. The 2nd, 9th, 29th, 1st and 2nd Canadian Divisions crossed the Rhine and occupied the bridge-head. We had a hectic time getting offices fixed up and trying to make things more comfortable for the troops. We were not allowed to buy food in Germany owing to fear of famine and ours had to come from Boulogne—parcels were looted *en route* and mails were frequently late. Owing to the nature of the ground, it was impossible to get football fields and hard to keep the men amused as they were mostly in bad billets in small villages. It was still impossible to get fresh clothing from the base and many of the men and officers were verminous and, naturally, most of them grousing. All our extra stores were held up and we thought it would be impossible to get anything through for the men for Christmas, but sent lorries to Paris and managed to get hold of pigs, turkeys, etc., in time. The chief trouble was that we could not get trains through, owing to the French repatriating the bombarded villages and towns and trying to put back machinery into the looted works as soon as possible.

Dec. 26th. The Germans had only food for eight weeks left and were, undoubtedly, very hard up—no raw material was allowed across the Rhine and manufacturers had to shut down. Games and amusements were gradually organised, but demobilisation caused a lot of trouble largely owing to the English Press; everybody thought they should be demobilised at once and I among them; that there was not any serious trouble in our area either with our own troops or civilian population was largely due to the old 'chief's' marvellous tact.

Some extracts of letters to his wife during this time are interesting. On the 20th May he writes:

Our airmen have been doing great things. Here in the

Second Army, we have destroyed 39 German planes in 3 days.

On the 24th he writes:

We had a useful little operation last night and took 40 prisoners: it all helps.

On the 27th he says:

We had a good little show last night, carried out I am glad to say by a battalion of the York and Lancaster Regiment.

The Duke of Connaught came over on the 30th and they had quite a nice little ceremony when he presented decorations to French officers. On 2nd July the duke again was with them, and returned to England the next day. On the 3rd July he says he was giving some military medals to some F.A.N.Y.'s who had most gallantly taken away the wounded during a bombing raid.

The same day he writes;

I have just heard the Australians in the South have carried out a first-rate show, and captured 1,000 prisoners, and the French have had an equally good one.

On the 12th he writes:

The Australians here did a very good operation yesterday and brought in almost 120 prisoners.

The next day, 13th July, he says:

The operations up here yesterday and the day before were quite good. We got about 200 prisoners and very few casualties.

On the 14th he says:

We had a success yesterday. The 6th Division took some ground we wanted and over 280 prisoners, a very good performance. I am very glad it was done by British troops.

On the 20th he says:

We had a very good small show yesterday. We took back

Meteren (or rather what used to be Meteren, because there is nothing left of the villages), and about 400 prisoners.

On the 30th the Australians had a successful show, taking 169 prisoners, and very few casualties. On the 6th August he writes:

The king came over yesterday, and went first to one of the Clearing Casualty stations where I met him. He looks very well and is in good spirits. Keppel, Stamfordham and Cromer are with him. He is spending a long day with us today. I only hope it will be fine, but it looks doubtful."

However, later he writes:

The weather has been on the whole kind. He saw troops most of the morning in an informal way and finished up with a small parade, when he presented 3 V.C.'s and my G.C.B.

On the 9th he reports the success in the south when the Canadian and Australian Corps got over 7,000 prisoners and 100 guns, and the French 2,500. It was a complete surprise, the secret very well kept, and altogether, from all accounts, some 27,000 prisoners. He writes:

The king is still here. H.M. has indeed brought us luck. He is coming to our church service tomorrow.

On the 18th August he writes just a line to say;

De Lisle's Corps had a very successful operation yesterday. We got all the ground we wanted and 670 prisoners.

On the 27th he says:

We had another little show last night, not many prisoners but all the ground we wanted. It all helps.

On the 26th he says that the chief of the Belgian Staff came to lunch. On the 31st:

The Germans have fallen back and we have got back

Kemmel and other places. We do not know how far they mean to go. I quite expected them to give up Bailleul, but I did not think they would give up Kemmel without a fight. However, it is a very good thing for us.

On the 1st September he writes:

We are making some progress, but we are not getting on as fast as I should like.

The next day they moved back to their old H.Q., which pleased them all.

On the 4th he reports that the progress though slow was steady. They got back Nieppe on the 3rd and then on to Lys. The next day he says he said goodbye to the other American general.

I am sorry they are going and they are sorry to go. They are full of life and consequently attractive.

On the 5th September he says:

We got on pretty well yesterday. De Lisle took Plogstadt village and Hill 60. We had some stiff fighting and we have not much to push with. Things are going very well. The Germans are going back pretty fast in front of the French and in front of our Fourth Army, and more slowly in front of our Third Army. I am delighted Fergusson was specially mentioned.

On the 12th he writes:

I am sorry to say we are losing Robertson from here. He is going to G.H.Q.: it is promotion for him and better pay, and it is work for which his leg will not affect him, so it is a good thing for him in every way, but I shall be sorry to lose him. He is one of the old lot and has worked here with us all the time.

On the 16th he writes:

The King of the Belgians asked me to go and see him

yesterday afternoon; he was very pleasant as he always is.

On the 25th;

> The Belgians and ourselves are attacking today. We started at 5.30. I am under the King of the Belgians for these operations. He (the king) came to tea yesterday, in very good spirits.

Later he says:

> We had a good day yesterday, a good deal better than I thought or expected—2,000 prisoners. The Belgians came along like anything, got 4,000 prisoners and all or nearly all the ground we were out to get.

The next he writes:

> We have got across the Messines and Wytschaete Ridge, now we ought to get on. It is such a relief.

Then:

> I don't expect you will get much news of our doings; as we are under the King of the Belgians we do not figure in the British *communiqué*, and the Belgians are naturally full of their own doings.

On 1st October he writes:

> The weather was very bad all day yesterday: we got on pretty well considering all things. We are up to Comines and Wervicq on the river and pretty close to Menin. As you can imagine, we have not a superfluity of troops, and a day like yesterday takes a good lot out of them. However, they have done and are doing very well, and everyone is doing their utmost. The Second Army has taken some 3,500 prisoners and pretty well 100 guns. Our casualties the first day were extraordinarily light. We, of course, have had more since.

On the 14th he writes;

We, the Belgians and the French are attacking this morning. It is a fine morning and I believe everything started all right.

Later:

Our operations seem to be going all right. We have got 900-odd prisoners so far.

Still later on the same day:

It has been a good day: we have done very well—the Second Army alone has taken 3,500 prisoners and about 50 guns. The French took 2,500, the Belgians 3,000.

The next day he says:

We are attacking again this morning, but not on a large scale.

The same evening, he says:

We have advanced our line a good bit. The troops have done very well.

The next day he says:

This morning we finished our present job in clearing all the ground north of the River Lys. I have been today to see the King of the Belgians and the staff—all very pleased and complimentary.

On the 18th he writes:

It was a great day yesterday: Birdwood got into Lille, the Belgians got into Ostend and the outskirts of Bruges. The admiral (Keyes) got into the harbour and landed himself.

On the 23rd he says:

Foch came here this morning, he was extraordinarily complimentary. You would have liked to have heard the nice things he said. He can be very charming.

On the 24th they moved their H.Q., as the old ones were

too far off from the corps commanders. On the 28th he writes:

> We carried out an attack yesterday to try and get nearer
> the Scheldt. We had some pretty hard fighting all day: the
> Second Army have had continuous fighting since the 28th
> September.

On the 31st they had what he calls a good day:

> We got 600 to 700 prisoners, and we got all the ground
> we went out to get.

On 1st November he says:

> We finished up well yesterday and got over 900 prisoners
> and a few guns. We are going on again today to square up,
> but as far as the Second Army is concerned, we have done
> all we were supposed to do this side of the Scheldt.

The next day he says:

> Our prisoners amounted to 1,125, our casualties were
> very light. The troops are all very pleased with themselves.

He came over on the night of the 12th for five days. He had
not been in England for over a year, for when he was coming,
he was sent off to Italy and after his return to the Second Army
he could not leave. He returned on the 19th.

They moved to Namur on the 23rd. On the 22nd he rode
into Brussels with the king and queen. He says:

> They had a wonderful reception, really magnificent. It was
> a most spontaneous exhibition of personal devotion to the
> king and queen. The king and queen rode first, followed
> by their two sons and their daughter and our Prince Al-
> bert. I rode just behind with the French general.

On the 28th he heard that King George, who was coming to
see the troops would not be able to come to the Second Army
at all. He was very disappointed for the sake of the troops, but it
made things easier for the move. He writes.:

> We shall probably go to Spa on Saturday. The corps that

will go into Germany are the II (Jacob) with the 9th, 29th and New Zealand Divisions, the Canadians (Currie) with the 1st and 2nd Canadian Divisions, the VI (Haldane) with the Guards 3rd and 2nd Divisions and the IX (Braithwaite) with the 1st, 6th and 62nd Division.

On the 29th he writes:

I think I told you that Sir Charles Fergusson is to be the Military Governor of Cologne. I am very glad; he will be a great help. We start for Spa early tomorrow morning. I am going to see the cavalry on my way.

The following is the message he received from the king who was then visiting the troops:

I cannot leave Flanders without letting you know how sorry I am not to have been able to visit the Second Army and personally to congratulate you on its triumphs. During the past few days, I have visited with pride and admiration the scenes of the famous battles with which the name of the Second Army will ever be associated. Rest assured that I follow with keen interest the daily onward march of your Columns and I trust that all ranks will soon be comfortably settled in their winter quarters.

George R.I.

★★★★★★★★★★

I find this telegram was not sent until the 9th of December when he writes: "I have just had the enclosed delightful telegram from the king. I am sending it to you at once. I know you will like to keep it."

★★★★★★★★★★

On the 4th December he writes from Spa;

I had to interview a German general, Von Winterfeldt, about sending troops to Cologne ahead of the others. So far only the cavalry have crossed the frontier (the infantry cross tomorrow). I was at a place called Montjoie yesterday where the cavalry are. So far, the attitude of the in habitants is a sort of studied indifference combined with curiosity.

I think we shall move our headquarters forward about the 8th or 9th to a place called Duren which is about half-way between here and Cologne.

Later on, he writes:

It is a great honour to be the Army of Occupation, but it carries a good many penalties with it. I can see it will not be a bed of roses by any means. It has turned out a dreadfully wet day and all our troops are on the march getting wet through. One of the trains of supplies has broken down again, and the 1st Canadian Division will have to halt again tomorrow. All very tiresome. However, the war is over and men are not being killed.

On the 9th he writes from Duren:

We arrived here yesterday morning: it took us about 3 hours by motor. We did not pass through a very interesting country, a manufacturing district, coal, etc. Fergusson will go into Cologne tomorrow as Military Governor. They seem quiet enough there. We have got cavalry and infantry all round it. I want to keep the troops as far as possible out of the town itself.

(It was at this time that he received the telegram from the king.)

On the 12th he writes:

The weather was not very kind to us today, but it might have been worse, and though it did come on to rain it did not begin until nearly all the troops had passed. I admit I was thrilled. The 2nd and 9th Cavalry Brigades marched through Cologne across the Rhine this morning. I and the Staff and Kavanagh and Jacob stood at the entrance of the Hohenzollern Bridge by the *Kaiser's* Statue, and at 10 o'clock the Union Jack was unfurled and the troops commenced to cross. The Band of the Blues played them past, men and horses looked splendid. They took about

101

1¾ hours to pass.

Tomorrow the infantry go across. Fergusson will see the 9th Division cross by this bridge, Jacob and I will see the 29th and then I go on and see the 1st Canadian Division and Currie sees the 2nd Canadian. Each division will take 4 to 5 hours to cross.

He writes as follows about the entry of the other troops into Cologne:

The march of the infantry and artillery across the Rhine yesterday was marred as a spectacle by the rain, which continued all day: it was very hard luck on the men as they had taken an immense amount of trouble to turn out well, and notwithstanding the weather they looked wonderfully well. They went over four bridges, starting at 9.30 and were not over till after 3, so the people of Cologne saw some troops.

He came over with Sir Douglas and they drove from Victoria to Buckingham Palace, and were given a tremendous welcome from the crowd. The ten days passed very quickly, and on the 31st he was back in Cologne. He writes:

Things seem very quiet here and nothing much seems to have happened.

He took part in the Victory March through London with Sir Douglas Haig and the other army commanders. They had a great reception.

The Third Battle of Ypres

By John Buchan

MESSINES

The Battle of Arras had died down before the end of May. Sir Douglas Haig, having protracted the fighting in that area so long as the French on the Aisne required his aid, was now free to turn his attention to the plan which as early as November 1916 had been his main objective. This was an offensive against the enemy forces in Flanders, with the aim of clearing the Belgian coast and turning the northern flank of the whole German defence system in the West. It was a scheme which, if successful, promised the most profound and far-reaching results. It would destroy the worst of the submarine bases; it would return to Belgium her lost territory, and thereby deprive the enemy of one of his cherished bargaining assets; it would cripple his main communications with the depots of the Lower Rhineland.

It offered the chance of a blow at a vital spot within a reasonable time. It was true that conditions had changed since the plan was first matured. The two months' conflict at Arras had used up a certain part of the British reserves. More important, the disastrous turn of the Russian situation had enabled the Germans to add greatly to their strength both in munitions and in men. Time, therefore, was the essence of the business. The blow must be struck at the earliest possible hour, for delay meant aggrandisement for the enemy.

But if the prize for success was high, the difficulties of the enterprise were great. For twelve months the front between the sea and the Lys had been all but stagnant. It had been for the first

103

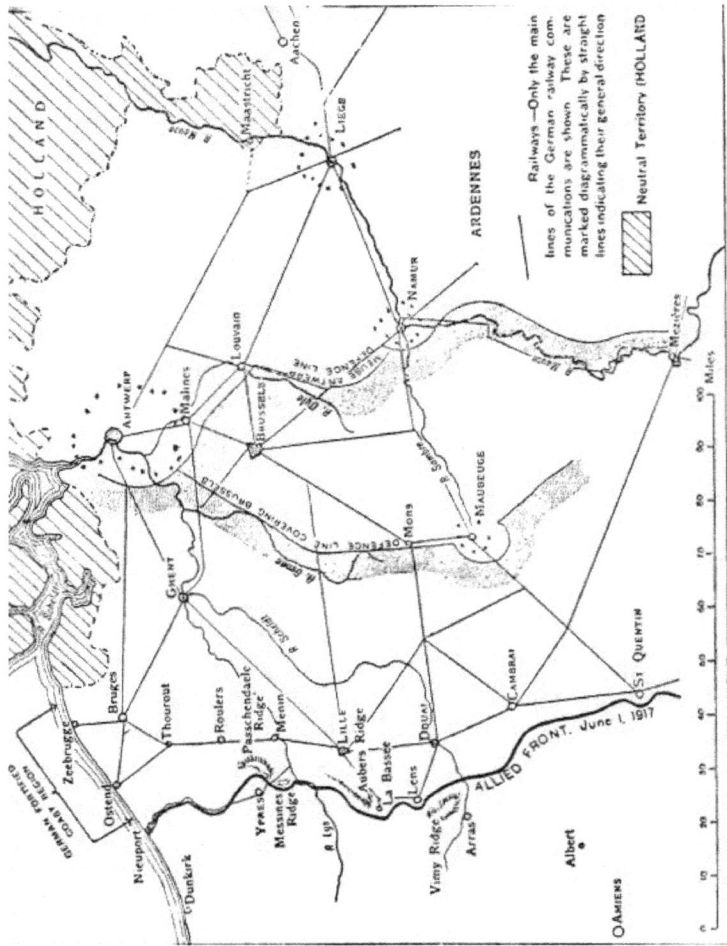

Sketch Map showing the strategic situation on the eve of the
Flanders Offensive of 1917.

two years the chief cockpit of British arms, and the enemy had spent infinite ingenuity and labour on perfecting his defences. In the half-moon of hills round Ypres and the ridge of Wytschaete and Messines he had view-points which commanded the whole countryside, and especially the British line within the Salient. (The extreme insignificance of these hills should be remembered. Ypres itself is 82 feet above the sea, so Wytschaete's 260 feet of height does not represent much compared to the general level of the country).

Any preparations for attack would be conducted under his watchful eye. Moreover, the heavy, water-logged clay of the flats where our front lay was terribly at the mercy of weather, and in rain became a bottomless swamp. Any attack must be in the position of a horseman taking a stiff fence from a bad jumping-off ground. Lastly, the Germans were acutely conscious of the importance of the terrain, and there was little chance of taking them by surprise.

In the beginning of June, the enemy in the Ypres area lay as follows. North of Ypres he was west of the canal between Steenstraat and Boesinghe. East of Ypres his front curved in a shallow arc, following the high ground called the Pilckem Ridge, by Wieltje and Hooge, which was the westernmost of the low tiers of hill which enclosed the Salient. From Observatory Ridge south of Hooge his line turned south-westward by Mount Sorrel and Hill 60 across the Ypres-Comines Canal to the point just south of the hamlet of St. Eloi. It then became a rounded salient, following the western skirts of the promontory formed by the Wytschaete-Messines Ridge. At the south end of this ridge, it turned eastward down the valley of the Steenebeek, crossed the Douve, and passed east of St. Yves to the banks of the Lys.

The apex of the Ypres Salient had been Becelaere in October 1914; in April 1915 it had been Broodseinde; and by the end of the Second Battle of Ypres it had contracted to Verlorenhoek and Hooge. During subsequent fighting it had shrunk still further, so that now the enemy front was only some two miles from the town. Not only was the eastern high ground wholly in the enemy's hands, but at the southern re-entrant Hill 60 gave

him direct observation over the Salient, and the Wytschaete-
Messines Ridge commanded Ypres itself, and every yard of the
British positions. The village of Wytschaete stood 260 feet high
on the loftiest point, and Messines, at the south end of the ridge,
gave a prospect over the Lys valley and enfiladed the British
lines on the Douve. If Sir Douglas Haig intended to break out
from the Salient, he must first clear the Germans off the southern ridges. Till that was achieved the British would be fighting
blindly against an enemy with a hundred eyes.

In June the German front from the sea to the Oise was held
by the Army group of the Bavarian Crown Prince. The Duke of
Wurtemberg had now gone south to the Vosges, and the Fourth
Army, from the coast to the Douve, was under General Sixt von
Armin, who had commanded the 4th Corps at the Somme, and
had shown himself one of the most original and fruitful tacti-
cians on the German side. South of him lay the Sixth Army,
under Otto von Below, the right wing of which extended for a
little way north of the Lys. Von Armin expected an assault even
before our bombardment began, and he rightly diagnosed that
its terrain would be the Messines Ridge. There lay the 4th German Corps, and on 1st June its commander, General von Laffert,
issued an order to his troops which accurately defined the limits
of the British attack. He ordered that all measures designed for
defence and counter-attack should be carefully tested.

All the reserves of the divisions attacked (with the exception of the emergency garrisons) will be at the absolute
disposal of those divisions for the purpose of repelling the
attack. Plentiful and well-advanced fighting reserves of the
army group will permit of the continuous bringing up of
other divisional reserves for an immediate powerful counter-attack. . . . The absolute retention of the natural strong
points of Wytschaete and Messines becomes of the utmost
importance for the domination of the whole Wytschaete
salient. These strong points, therefore, must not fall, even
temporarily, into the enemy's hands. Both must be defended to the utmost, and held to the last man, even if the

enemy has cut the connection on both sides and threatens the strong points from the rear. The troops must be told that we have very strong battle reserves close behind the front, which are destined to throw back any enemy who may have temporarily broken through, in our great counter-attack, should the battle reserves of the division not already have done so.

Von Armin was anxious but confident. He had a position strong by nature, and enormously fortified by art. He had ample reserves of men, and he had brought up many new batteries, which were disposed mainly north and south of the Wytschaete salient, so as to enfilade any British advance and be themselves safe from capture. He had a number of new anti-tank guns, and in the flattish ground at each end of the ridge he experimented in the construction of those concrete "pill-boxes" which were later to prove so serious an obstacle to the British advance from Ypres. His plan was to hold his front line lightly, but to have strong reserves in rear to defend any position of importance. Behind these were his battle reserves, to be used for counter-attacks; for his tactical policy was to trust to counter-attack before the enemy had secured his ground, rather than to fight desperately for every yard.

For such tactics it was essential that the moment of the real offensive should be instantly grasped, and if possible foreseen. The reserves must be moved at once; but it would be fatal if they were moved because of a feint, for in that case they would fall under our barrage and be depleted before the time had come for their use. Von Armin had judged rightly about the terrain; but, as it happened, he could not define the hour. In no British attack had Sir Douglas Haig succeeded in concealing the *locale*; but in all he had perplexed the enemy as to the exact time of assault.

The British front was held by the Second Army, which had not altered its position since the spring of 1915. The First Army had fought at Festubert, and had borne the brunt of Loos. The Fourth and Fifth Armies had conducted the Battle of the

Somme. The First, Third, and Fifth Armies had been engaged at Arras. But the last great action of the Second Army had been Second Ypres. It had seen much bitter fighting in 1916 round Hooge and the Bluff; but it had taken no part as an army in any major battle, though its divisions had been drawn upon for the Somme and Arras. To hold a long front not actively engaged, and to provide reinforcements for other armies, is one of the most difficult duties which can fall to the lot of a general. Corporate unity seems to have gone from his command, and it needs patience and resolution to keep up that vigilance and *esprit de corps* which are essential in war.

The Second Army was fortunate in its leader. Sir Herbert Plumer, now sixty years of age, had in the highest degree the traditional virtues of the British soldier, and especially of those county line regiments which have always been the backbone of the British Army. He had fought with his regiment, the York and Lancaster, in the Sudan in 1884; he had served in the Matabele rebellion; in the South African War he had contributed to the relief of Mafeking, had taken Pietersburg, and had hunted De Wet in the Cape Colony. At the Second Battle of Ypres, he had shown a rapidity of decision and an imperturbability of temper which had turned the tide in that grim encounter.

But his most brilliant work had been accomplished during the long months of comparative inaction which followed. He had been a true warden of the Flanders marches, and had watched over every mile of that front, so that our energy in defence and in the minor offensives of trench warfare never slackened. Assisted by a most competent staff, he had inspired throughout his army a complete trust in their leader, and had welded all types—old Regulars, Territorials, New Army—into one tempered weapon. There were no jealousies under his command, and every man in it knew that competence and faithfulness would be recognized and rewarded. Moreover, for a year and more Sir Herbert Plumer had been making ready for the offensive in which he was to play the chief part. Methodical and patient preparation had been carried by him to the pitch of genius.

To understand the battle, it is necessary to examine more closely the topography of the Wytschaete-Messines ridge. Seen from the western hills, such as Kemmel, behind the British lines, it appeared to be an inconsiderable slope merging in the north in the low ridges east of Ypres, but breaking down in the south to the Lys valley in a steeper gradient. The landmarks on it were the ruins of the White Château at Hollebeke, the dust-heap which once was Wytschaete village, and the tooth of the ruined church of Messines. Viewed from below, from the British trenches in the marshy flats of the Steenebeek, it was more imposing—a low hillside seamed with white trenches, and dotted with the debris of old woods—a bald, desolated height, arid as a brickfield, rising from the rank grass and yellow mustard of No Man's Land. The German first-line trenches curved along the foot of the slope, and their second line system made an inner curve on the crest of the ridge.

To the north the Germans held Hill 60 and the Mound at St. Eloi, and had constructed strong fortifications in the grounds of the White Château, and along the road called the Damm Strasse which led from Hollebeke to Wytschaete. But, as in all salients, the most important defence was the chord which cut the arc—what the Germans called *Sehnenstellung*—and which was intended as the rear defence should the front of the Salient be carried. The third German system was such a chord, running from Mount Sorrel in the north, a little east of the village of Oosttaverne, to Gapaard in the south. This line was the proper base of the Salient. A mile east of it lay the fourth and final German position in that area, which reached the Lys at the town of Warneton.

The Oosttaverne line was the British objective in the action, for its capture would mean that the Salient had gone and the whole ridge was in our hands. To reach it the enemy front must be penetrated to a depth of two and a half miles. Its length was about six miles; but if the curve of the main salient was followed, without reckoning the many minor salients and re-entrants, the whole battle frontage was nearly ten. It should be remembered, too, that, apart from the main enemy lines, the whole western face of the ridge, and all the little woods to the north and

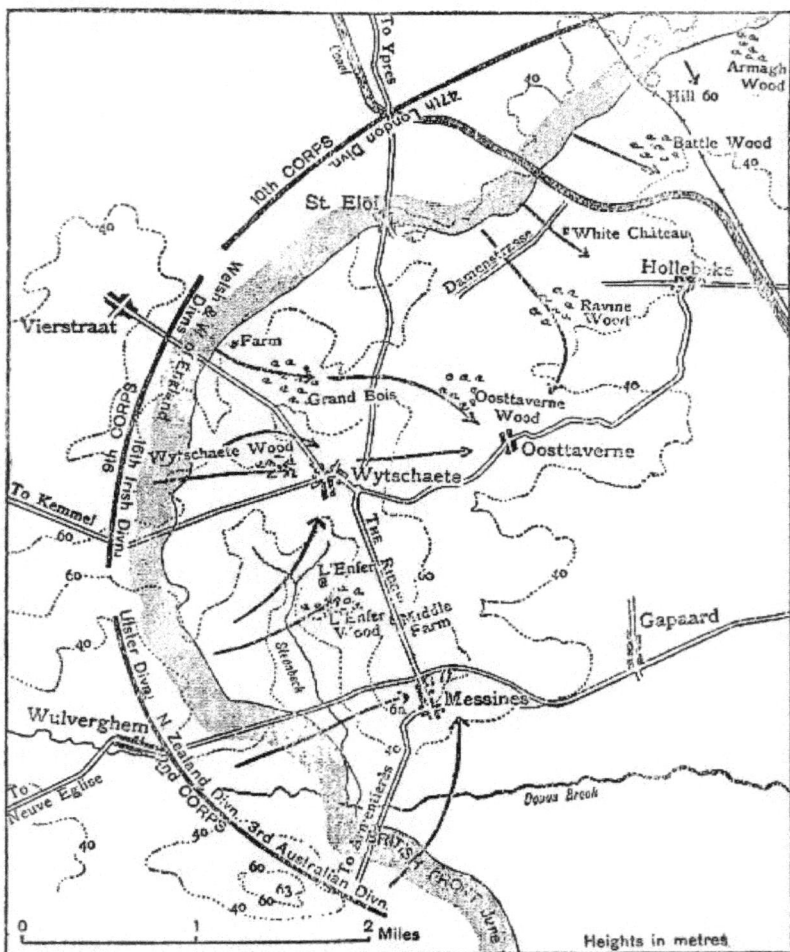

Sketch showing general scheme of the attack on the Messines-Wytschaete Ridge.

north-west, were a maze of skilfully sited trenches and redoubts, designed to bring flanking fire to bear upon any ground won by the attack. The British front of assault was held by three of the six corps of the Second Army.

From opposite Mount Sorrel, astride the Ypres–Comines Canal to the Grand Bois just north of Wytschaete, lay the 10th Corps, under General Morland, with a north-country division on its extreme left, and the 47th London Division in the centre. Opposite Wytschaete was the 9th Corps, under General Hamilton-Gordon, containing Welsh and West of England troops and the 16th Irish Division. South lay the 2nd Anzac Corps, under General Godley, with the Ulster Division on its left, the New Zealand Division as its centre, and the 3rd Australian Division on its right astride the Douve. The two southern corps had the task of the direct assault on the ridge, while the loth Corps, with a much longer front, had to clear the hillocks towards the Ypres Salient, and advance upon the ridge and the Oosttaverne line from its northern flank.

The Wytschaete-Messines Ridge had seen no fighting since the close of 1914. At the end of October in that year, during the First Battle of Ypres, Allenby's weary cavalry, assisted by Indian and British infantry, had made for two days a gallant stand at Messines before they were forced into the flats. In December a combined attack had been made by French and British troops on the woods of Petit Bois and Maedelsteed, west of Wytschaete, but the position had proved too strong to carry. Thereafter, while the battle had raged as near as St. Eloi in the north and Fromelles in the south, the Messines area had been an enclave of quiet. But for nearly two years an offensive had been going on underground.

As early as July 1915 it had been resolved to make use of the clay *stratum* below our position for extensive mining operations, and in January 1916 we had gone seriously to work. We used in our tunnelling companies some of the best expert talent in the world, men who in private life had received huge salaries from mining corporations. It was work attended by endless difficulties and dangers. Water-bearing *strata* would suddenly be encountered, which necessitated damming and pumping work on a big scale. The enemy was busy countermining, and we had to be ever on the watch to detect his progress, and by *camouflets* (mines with a small charge, intended only to destroy an enemy shaft, and not to make a crater), to blow in his galleries. At some points the struggle was continuous and desperate, especially after February 1, 1917. At the Bluff, for instance, between January 16, 1916, and June 7, 1917, twenty-seven *camouflets* were blown, seventeen by the British and ten by the enemy. The Spanbroekmolen mine, south-west of Wytschaete, had its gallery destroyed; for three months it was cut off, and only reopened by a great effort the day preceding the Messines attack. But the most dramatic case was that of Hill 60. To quote the official report:—

> At Hill 60 continuous underground fighting took place for over ten months prior to our attack, and only by the greatest skill, persistence, and disregard of danger on the part of our tunnellers were the two mines laid by us at this point saved from destruction. At the time of our offensive the enemy was known to be driving a gallery which ultimately would have cut into the gallery leading to the Hill 60 mine. By careful listening it was judged that if our offensive took place on the date arranged the enemy's gallery would just fail to reach us. So, he was allowed to proceed.

In all we dug twenty-four mines, and some of these were ready a year before the attack. We constructed some five miles of galleries, and charged them with over a million pounds of ammonal. Four were outside the front ultimately selected for our attack, and one was destroyed by the enemy. But on the evening of 6th June nineteen were waiting for zero hour.

The preparation was not confined to underground. Road and railway communications had been improved throughout the whole area. In order to provide water for our advance the various lakes and ponds behind the line were tapped; cisterns to catch rain water were constructed on the Kemmel hills; and the water of the Lys was pumped into barges and sterilized. From these sources pipe lines were carried forward to the front, and provision was made for their rapid extension after the attack. The consequence was that troops could be supplied with water half an hour or so after winning their objective—no slight boon in a battle fought in the height of summer.

Again, from the last days of May a pitiless bombardment had assailed the enemy area, devastating his front line and searching out his rear positions. The last remnants of Wytschaete and Messines villages disappeared. The woods on the slopes ceased to be tattered, and became fields of stumps. In that hot, dry weather a cloud of dust hung all day long about the slopes, and at night they blazed like the boulevard of a great city. Our raiding activity was unceasing, and from the dazed prisoners and from many captured letters we learned of the miseries of the enemy. Certain Irish troops made five distinct raids in forty hours. British aircraft spent their days over the German hinterland, and prevented any enemy planes from learning the extent of our preparation.

"Our machines never even get so far as our front lines," wrote a German officer. In one fight five British planes encountered twenty-seven German, wrecked eight, and returned safely home. Between 1st June and 6th June, we destroyed twenty-four enemy machines, and drove down twenty-three out of control, at the cost of ten of our own.

On the evening of Wednesday, 6th June, the weather broke in a violent thunderstorm. Torrents of rain fell, and from the baked earth rose a warm mist which folded the ground like a cloak. During the night the heavens were overcast, so that the full moon was not seen, and only a luminous glow told of its presence. But at 2.30 a.m. on the 7th the skies cleared, the moon rode out, and to a watcher on the hills to the west the whole landscape stood forth in a sheen made up of moonlight and the foreglow of dawn.

Our bombardment had abated, but during the night the enemy had grown nervous. He had sent up rockets and flames calling for a barrage, and his guns began to pour forth shrapnel and high explosives. Somewhere north of Wytschaete a dump had caught fire, and poured forth tongues of red flame. As the dawn broadened our guns seemed to cease, though the enemy's were still active. The air was full of the hum of our bombing and reconnoitring planes flying eastward, and our balloons were going up—tawny patches against the June sky. Then came a burst of German high explosives, and then, at precisely ten minutes past three, a sound compared to which all other noises were silence.

From Hill 60 in the north to the edge of Messines, with a shock that made the solid earth quiver like a pole in the wind, nineteen volcanoes leaped to heaven. Nineteen sheets of flame seemed to fill the world. For a moment it looked as if the earth, under a magician's wand, had been contorted into gigantic toadstools. The black cloud-caps seemed as real as the soil beneath them. Then they shook and wavered and thinned, leaving a brume of dust, rosy and golden atop with the rising sun.

And at the same moment, while the ears were still throbbing with the concussion of the mines, every British gun opened on the enemy. Flashes of many colours stabbed the wall of dust, the bursts of shrapnel stood out white against it, and smoke barrages from our trenches burrowed into its roots. The sun was now above the horizon, and turned the fringes of the cloud to a hot purple and crimson. No battle had ever a more beautiful and terrible staging. And while the debris of the explosion still hung in the air the British divisions of assault went over their parapets.

They entered at once upon a world like the nether pit—poisonous with gas fumes, twisted and riven out of all character, a maze of quarried stone, moving earth, splintered concrete, broken wire, and horrible fragments of humanity. In most places the German front lines had been blown out of existence. A few nerve-shattered survivors were taken prisoner in the dug-outs that had escaped destruction, and here and there a gallant machine-gun officer, who had miraculously survived, obeyed his orders till death took him. Let us follow from south to north the progress of the British advance.

The 3rd Australian Division, facing the extreme right of Otto von Below's Sixth Army, pushed across the Douve on duckboard bridges, and, assisted by a tank drove the enemy by the early afternoon from the southern slopes of the Messines Ridge. This safeguarded our right flank, and enabled the New Zealand Division to move securely on Messines village. The latter swarmed across the Steenebeek and climbed the hill on the side where the Armentières road dipped to the flats. A little after five the smoke had cleared sufficiently to show them the skyline to the north and the men of the Ulster Division silhouetted there. The New Zealanders, fighting their way in from the south, cleared Messines by seven o'clock. They were now reinforced by the 4th Australians, who moved on to the redoubt called Fanny's Farm, half a mile to the north-east. A tank cleared out the garrison, and by midday the Second Anzac Corps had won their main objective.

Farther north the Ulster Division, which contained on its right a battalion of the Cheshires, had moved from the trenches north of Wulverghem against that part of the ridge which lay between Messines and Wytschaete. They had before them a peculiarly difficult problem. On the crest midway between the two villages ran the Bois de l'Enfer and the concrete fort of L'Enfer, and to the south another nest of redoubts which was known as Hell Farm. To reach the crest the division had to move down the exposed western slope of the Steenebeek valley, cross the stream, ascend the opposite slope, and carry the various Hell positions.

Beyond the crest were strong trench lines, and a bare open plateau all the way to Oosttaverne and Gapaard. From their starting-place it was 2,000 yards to the crest. The German position had been held by the 40th Saxons; but on the evening of the 6th June, they were relieved by the famous 3rd Bavarians, so that the Ulstermen had to face an unwearied and most gallant enemy.

During the night before the attack the Cheshires had moved into No Man's Land, and dug a trench for their starting-point next day. Hence the enemy barrage, when it began, fell behind them. The explosion of the Spanbroekmolen mine gave the division some cover when they raced down the Steenebeek slopes. Across the stream they rushed and up the ridge, and soon the Cheshires were at work among the Hell redoubts. By stern hand-to-hand fighting they cleared them out, and presently the whole division was on the crest line, where a broad highway linked Messines and Wytschaete. There they halted for reserves, and then swept through the trench system east of the road. Linked up with the Anzacs, they took Middle Farm and Despagne Farm, and by midday were up against the Oosttaverne line.

Wytschaete fell to the left wing of the Ulstermen, and the 16th (South Ireland) Division. Now were seen, for the first time for generations, Irish units, widely sundered by politics and creed, fighting in generous rivalry for a common cause. The first obstacle, the wood called Petit Bois, was wiped out of being by a mine explosion. The Irish drove on into Wytschaete Wood, tearing through the uncut wire, and overwhelming machine-gun nests by the sheer fury of their onset. By eight o'clock they were opposite the northern and western defences of Wytschaete, while the Ulstermen were waiting at the southern end of the village.

Long before noon the place was carried, and the Irish were moving down the road to Oosttaverne. In the early hours of the day this division had sustained a grievous loss. The brother of the Irish Nationalist leader, Major William Redmond, was hit by a shell fragment, and died a few hours later. Though far beyond military age, he had enlisted early in the war, and had loyally endured all the hardships of campaigning, which do not come easily to a man well advanced in middle life. He had striven all his days for Irish unity, and he had put his precepts most gallantly into practice. *Felix opportunitate mortis*, he had lived to see that union of spirit realised, if not in the dusty *coulisses* of politics, in the nobler arena of battle, and it was an Ulster ambulance that bore him from the field.

Meantime, on the left of the French and beyond the Wytschaete-Vierstraat road Welsh and West of England divisions were moving on the northern butt of the ridge. Starting from Hollandscheschuur Farm, the Welsh picked their way through the smoking mine craters, and, with the assistance of the West Countrymen, carried the Grand Bois. Soon they were over the crest and through the German second system beyond the Ypres-Armentières road. By midday they were fighting in Oosttaverne Wood, and early in the afternoon were on the edge of Oosttaverne itself.

On the British left the situation was more complex, for the

tactical problem was far less simple than the straightforward assault on the ridge. General Morland's 10th Corps had to fight astride a canal in a confused country of hillocks and ravines and nondescript woods. The extreme left, North England troops of the 23rd Division, had the easiest task. Around Mount Sorrel and Armagh Wood, the German front had been blown to pieces. Hill 60, with its elaborate defences, had virtually disappeared. Our losses were trifling, and one battalion won its objective with only ten casualties. But the Londoners of the 47th Division had a harder task. Few divisions had borne themselves more gallantly in the war, and Loos and High Wood were only two of their many battle honours.

They were held by machine-gun fire from the spoil banks on each side of the Ypres-Comines Canal; and, with English south-country troops on the right, had to fight for the strongholds of Ravine Wood and Battle Wood, the White Château, and the long, fortified line of the Damm Strasse. The last had been well broken up by our bombardment, but in the grounds and outbuildings of the *château* and around the dry lake there was sharp fighting. In Ravine Wood a Kentish battalion had a desperate bayonet struggle with part of the German 35th Division. By the early afternoon, however, the 10th Corps had gained its final objectives, with the exception of a small part of the eastern end of Battle Wood and a few strong points on the canal banks. The flank was therefore safe, and the British centre lay parallel to the Oosttaverne line, between 400 and 700 yards to the west of it.

Our guns had advanced, and the time had come for the final attack. It was launched about three o'clock, and at 3.45 the Welsh entered the village of Oosttaverne from the west. By four the English county troops on their left had taken the Oosttaverne line east of the village, and captured twelve guns. Before darkness fell the whole of the line was in our hands, and Sir Herbert Plumer had gained his final objective.

The counter-attack which von Armin had planned was slow to develop. On the afternoon of the 7th there was a small attempt on the right of our front, which was easily repulsed by the Australians. During the night we secured our gains, and on the

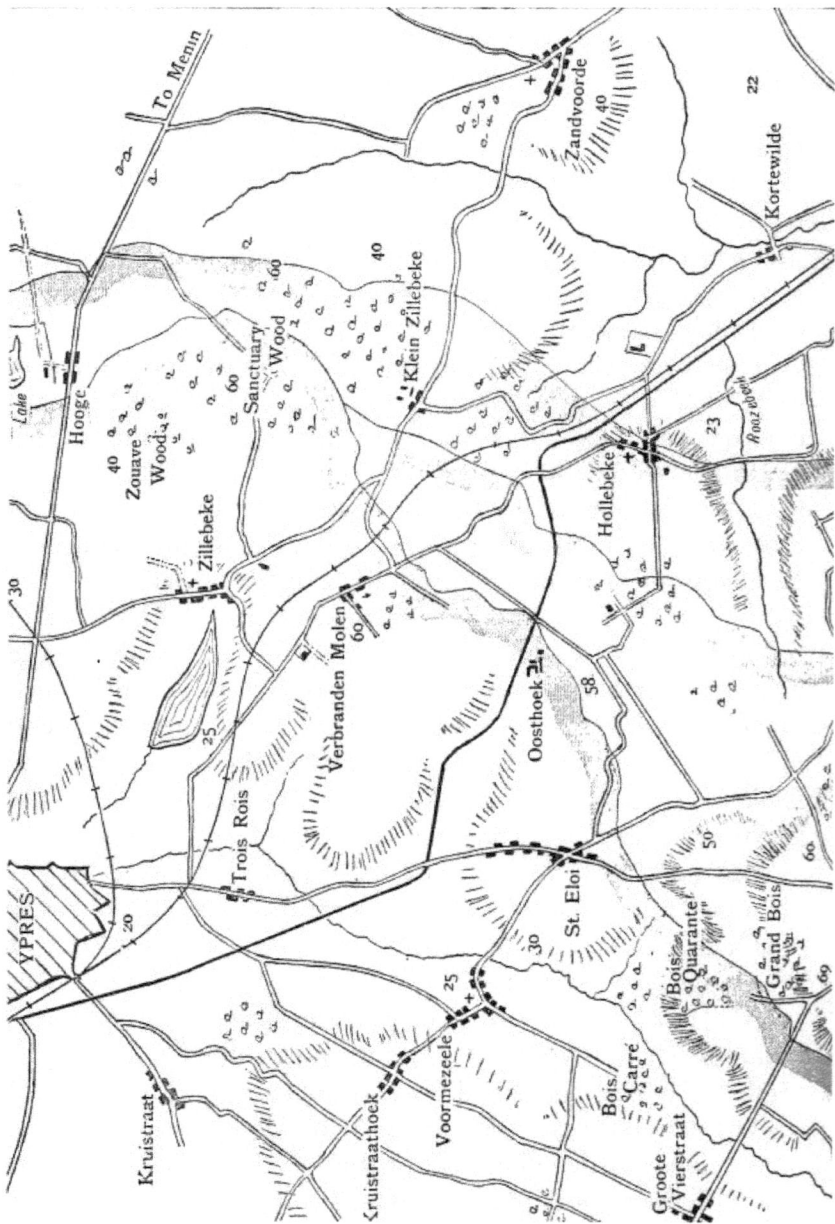

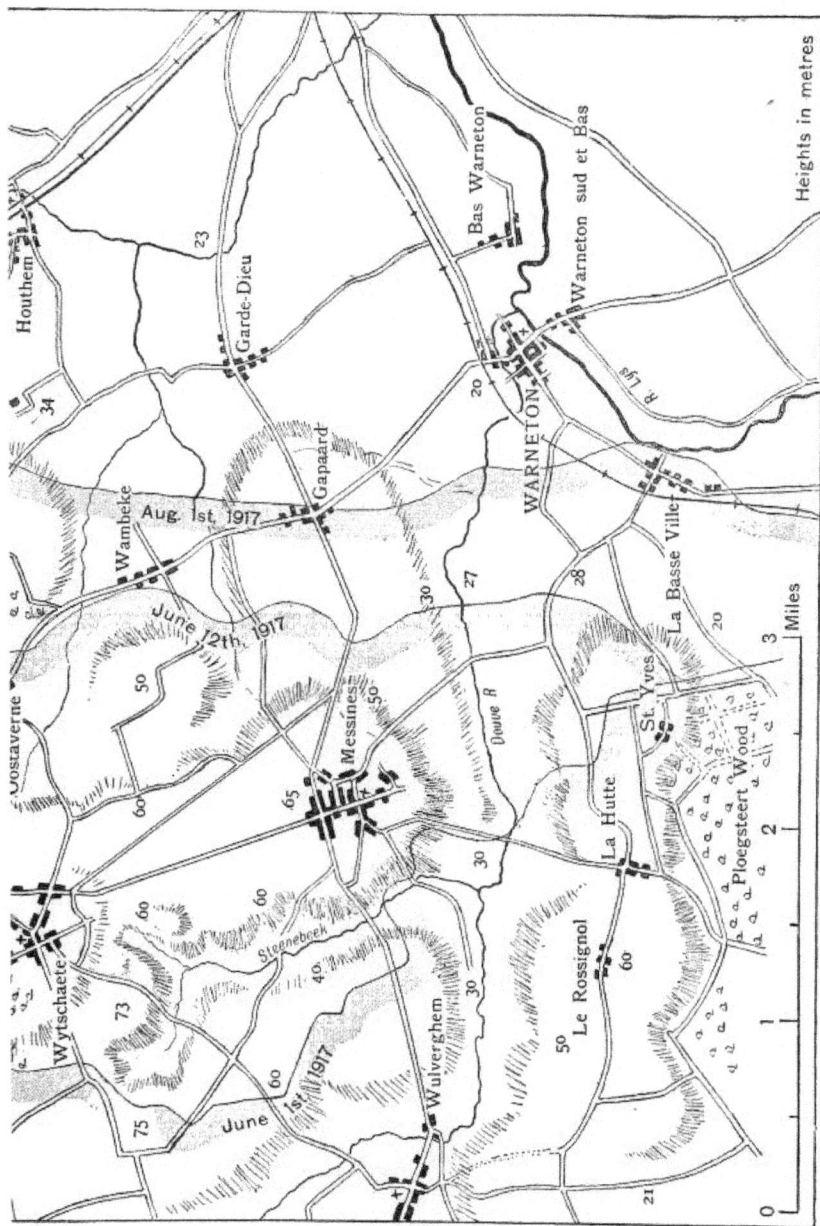

Heights in metres

Houthem

23

Garde-Dieu

Bas Warneton

Warneton sud et Bas

34

Gapaard

20

Wambeke

Aug. 1st, 1917

WARNETON

R. Lys

Oostaverne

June 12th, 1917

30

27

28

50

Messines

50

Douve R.

La Basse Ville

20

65

St. Yves

Wytschaete

60

60

30

La Hutte

Ploegsteert Wood

73

Steenebeek

40

Le Rossignol

60

75

60

Wulverghem

30

50

21

June 1st, 1917

0   1   2   3

Miles

morning of the 8th cleared up a few remaining lengths of German trench. Not till that evening was there any sign of a counterstroke. At 7 p.m., after an intense bombardment, the Germans attacked along nearly the whole length of our new line, and at every point were repulsed. The surprise and shock of the action of the 7th had been too great to permit of a speedy recovery. During the next few days, the Australians took the farm of La Potterie, little more than a mile west of Warneton, and the village of Gapaard, on the Ypres-Warneton road.

The position of the right wing of von Below's Sixth Army between St. Yves and the Lys was now untenable. It gradually withdrew to La Basse Ville, and by the 14th the whole of the old German positions north of the Lys, both front and support lines, had fallen into our hands. That evening we attacked again on both our flanks, clearing out some of the strong points north of the Ypres-Comines Canal, and forcing the enemy on the south back to the line of the River Warnave.

Sir Herbert Plumer's task had been brilliantly and fully accomplished. In a single day's fighting, he had advanced two and a half miles on a front of nearly ten; he had wiped out the German salient, and carried also its chord; he had stormed positions on the heights which the enemy regarded as impregnable; his losses were extraordinarily small, and he had taken 7,200 prisoners, 67 guns, 94 trench mortars, and 294 machine guns. The Battle of Messines will rank in history with Nivelle's two victories at Verdun, in the winter of 1916, as a perfect instance of the success of the limited objective. It could not be a normal type of battle. The elaborate preparation, the concentration of guns, and the careful rehearsal of every part demanded time and quiet which cannot be commonly reckoned on in war. But Sir Herbert Plumer had achieved what deserves to be regarded as in its own fashion a tactical masterpiece.

Meantime, in order to mask the preparations which were being made for the main enterprise of the summer—the breakout from the Ypres Salient—General Home's Third Army undertook various small offensives. On 14th June we carried by a surprise attack the enemy lines on the crest of Infantry Hill south-east of Arras, taking 175 prisoners in two minutes. On the 15th we took a sector of the Hindenburg Line north-east of Bullecourt. For some weeks Canadian and English troops had been active in the neighbourhood of Lens, and on the 24th the North Midland Division carried Hill 65, south-west of the town, forcing the enemy to withdraw on both sides of the Souchez River. On the 26th the Canadians took La Coulotte, and on the morning of the 28th were in the outskirts of Avion.

That evening General Home devised an ingenious bluff. Elaborate demonstrations were made by means of the discharge of gas and smoke to convince the enemy that he was about to be attacked on the twelve-mile front from Gavrelle to Hulluch, and a bogus raid was carried out southeast of Loos. The real attack was made on a front of 2,000 yards in front of Oppy, and by the Canadians and North Midlanders astride the Souchez River. We gained all our objectives, including the southern part of the ruins of Avion and the hamlet of Eleu dit Leauvette, on the Lens-Arras road, together with 300 prisoners and many machine guns. More important, we succeeded in puzzling the enemy as to what was the aim of our main offensive. Messines pointed to Lille as much as to Ypres, and the activity at Lens suggested that our aim might be to cut in to north and south of Lille, and wrest the great French industrial city from the enemy.

THE SALIENT AND PASSCHENDAELE

The Third Battle of Ypres was the residuum left to Sir Douglas Haig of the great plan of a Flanders offensive which he had conceived the previous winter. Events which he could not control had postponed it till too late in the summer. His preparation for it had been impeded time and again by the necessity of turning his attention to some other area. When at last his hands were free, there were certain special obstacles, the story of which cannot yet be told, which postponed the actual launching of the attack. The preliminary work of Messines was over by 12th June, but it was not till late in July that the day of the main advance was fixed. The delay meant that the enterprise was much canvassed in Germany, and the enemy line fully warned between Lille and the sea. The plan, as it was finally put into action, bristled with difficulties which might have deterred a less stout-hearted commander.

It was in some degree a race against time. If a true strategic purpose was to be effected before winter, the first stages must be quickly passed. The high ground east of the Salient must be won in a fortnight, to enable the British to move against the German bases in West Flanders and clear the coastline. Moreover, it was now evident that the Russian front was crumbling; already many divisions and batteries had come westward, and those left behind had been skimmed for shock-troops. Soon the process would proceed more rapidly, and the British would be faced with an accumulation of reserves strong enough to bar their way. Again, the nature of the terrain made any offensive a gamble with the weather. A dry autumn like that of 1914 would be well enough, but a repetition of the Somme experience must spell disaster.

The Salient was, after Verdun, the most tortured of the Western battlefields. Constant shelling of the low ground west of the ridges had blocked or diverted the streams and the natural drainage and turned it into a sodden wilderness. Much rain would make of it a morass where tanks could not be used, and transport could scarcely move, and troops would be exposed to the last degree of misery. Finally, as has already been pointed out, it was ill ground to debouch from; for though we had won the Messines heights, the enemy still held the slopes which, in semi-circular tiers, rise to the main ridge of Passchendaele, and had direct observation over all the land west to the canal and the ruins of Ypres. Whatever might be the strength and skill of the Germans, they were less formidable than the barriers which Nature herself might place in the British path.

But the commander of the German Fourth Army was no despicable antagonist. He had suffered a sharp defeat at Messines; but he had the type of mind which reacts against failure, and, as he had done a year before on the Somme, he set himself to adapt his defence to the British mode of attack. During the first half of 1917 the enemy's major plan had been that of retirement through various fortified zones. He was still strictly on the defensive, and his aim was to allow the Allies to waste their strength in making small territorial gains which had no real strategic value. He had successively lost all his most important observation points; but he had still on most parts of his front those immense entrenchments, constructed largely by the labour of Russian prisoners, which could only be captured piecemeal after a great expense of shells. In Flanders the nature of the ground did not permit of a second Siegfried Line. Deep dug-outs and concrete-lined trenches were impossible because of the water-logged soil, and he was compelled to find new tactics.

Von Armin's solution was the "pill-box" which we have already noted at Messines. These were small concrete forts, sited among the ruins of a farm or in some derelict piece of woodland, often raised only a yard or two above the ground level, and bristling with machine guns. The low entrance was at the rear, and the ordinary pill-box held from twenty to forty men. It was easy to make, for the wooden or steel framework could be brought up on any dark night and filled with concrete. They were echeloned in depth with great skill; and, in the wiring, alleys were left so that an unwary advance would be trapped among them and exposed to enfilading fire. Their small size made them a difficult mark for heavy guns, and since they were protected by concrete at least three feet thick, they were impregnable to the ordinary barrage of field artillery.

The enemy's plan was to hold his first line—which was often a mere string of shell-craters linked by a trench—with few men, who would fall back before an assault. He had his guns well behind, so that they should not be captured in the first rush, and would be available for a barrage when his opponents were entangled in the "pill-box" zone. Finally, he had his reserves in the second line, ready for the counterstroke before the attack could secure the ground won. It will be seen that these tactics were admirably suited for the exposed and contorted ground of the Salient. Any attack would be allowed to make some advance; but if the German plan worked well, this advance would be short-lived, and would be dearly paid for. Instead of the cast-iron front of the Siegfried area, the Flanders line would be highly elastic, but would spring back into position after pressure with a deadly rebound.

The new offensive involved a complete redistribution of the Allied forces. The front of the Third Army, under Sir Julian Byng, who had succeeded to Allenby's command, was greatly extended, and now covered all the ground between Arras and the junction with the French. This released Sir Hubert Gough's Fifth Army and Sir Henry Rawlinson's Fourth Army for service in the north. In early June French troops had held the front on the Yser between St. Georges and the sea. These were now relieved by the British Fourth Army. The Belgian forces on the canal drew in their right from Boesinghe to Noordschoote, and that section was occupied by the French First Army of three corps under General Anthoine, who had commanded the Sixth Army in spring in the Moronvilliers battle.

From Boesinghe to the Zillebeke-Zandvoorde road southeast of Ypres lay the British Fifth Army, and on its right the Second Army as far as the Lys. From Armentieres to Arras Sir Henry Home's First Army held the front. The main striking forces were Gough's and Anthoine's; but it was intended that Home should undertake, by way of distraction, certain movements against Lens, and that Plumer should threaten to the south of the Salient so as to compel the enemy to distribute his artillery fire.

The appearance of Rawlinson on the coast in the second half of June gravely alarmed the German command. It seemed to indicate an attack along the shore, assisted by our fleet at sea, which had long been a favourite subject of German speculation. They resolved to anticipate it by depriving the British of their bridgehead east of the canalised Yser. The dunes formed a belt of dry land along the coast about a mile wide, where movement was possible in any weather; but south of them lay a flat country criss-crossed with endless streams and ditches which could be easily flooded so as to bar the advance of an enemy. The Allied line, which from Dixmude northward lay on the west bank of the Yser, crossed to the east bank south of Nieuport. This gave us a bridge-end about two miles long, and from 600 to 1,200

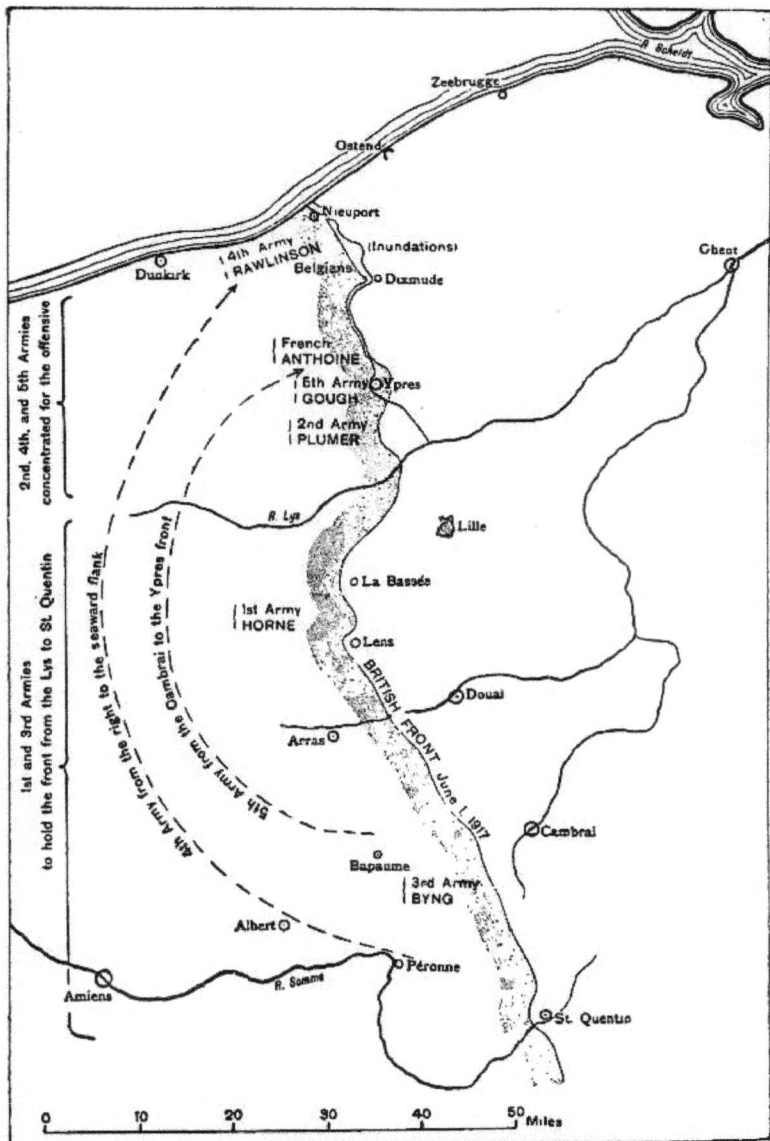

Regrouping of the British Armies for the Flanders Offensive, 1917.

yards deep, from the Plasschendaele Canal south of Lombartzyde to the sea. Half-way a dyke known as the Geleide Creek
intersected our front. If the enemy could drive us across the Yser,
he would have a stronger defensive position in the event of a
coastal advance.

Very early on the morning of Tuesday, 10th July, an intense
bombardment broke out against the bridgehead. There was a
heavy gale blowing, which probably accounted for the absence
of British naval support. In the dune and polder country trenches were impossible, and the British defence consisted of breast-
works built in the sand. These were speedily flattened out, and
all the bridges across the Yser north of the Geleide dyke were
destroyed, as well as the bridges over the dyke itself. The bombardment continued all day, and at 6.30 in the evening troops of
a German Naval Division advanced in three waves. The bridgehead between the Geleide Creek and the shore was held by two
battalions of the Northamptons and the King's Royal Rifles.

Since all communications were destroyed, they were unable
to fall back; and for an hour, against overwhelming numbers,
and in positions from which all cover had gone, they maintained
a most gallant defence. By eight o'clock the action was over,
and the two battalions had disappeared as units, though during that and the following night some seventy men and four
officers managed to swim the Yser and return to our lines. The
northern part of the bridgehead was captured; but south of the
Geleide dyke, opposite Lombartzyde, where our position had
greater depth, and some of the Yser bridges were still intact,
the assault was held, and the enemy driven out of our lines by a
counter-attack.

The affair was trivial and easily explicable: the bridgehead
was at the mercy of a sudden attack in force unless we had chosen to take very special measures to defend it. It was another instance of what the past two years had abundantly proved—that
any advanced trench system could be taken by the side which
was prepared to mass sufficient troops and guns.

Meantime through July the preparations for the great Salient
battle were being assiduously pressed on. The shell of Ypres did

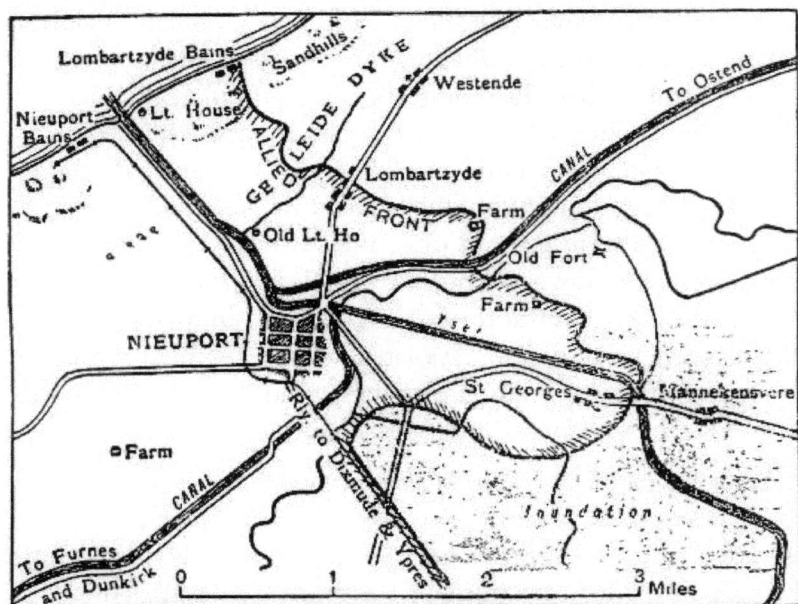

Scene of the German Attack near Nieuport.

not provide, either above ground or underground, the cover for the assembling of troops which Arras had afforded; consequently, the labours of our tunnelling companies were heavy and incessant. Our aircraft did marvellous work in locating enemy batteries, and our guns in destroying them. Of the latter arm the official dispatch tells a remarkable story:—

> A howitzer battery had received orders to cut a section of German wire in the neighbourhood of Hooge, and four hundred rounds had been allocated for the purpose. The battery, situated in an unavoidably exposed position in the neighbourhood of Zillebeke Lake, had already been subjected to constant shelling. On the occasion referred to, not more than fifty rounds had been fired at the German wire, when a hostile 15 cm. battery opened a steady and accurate fire in enfilade. Each time the British battery opened, salvos of 15 cm. shells raked its position. Four of its six guns were put out of action, and two ammunition dumps were blown up; but the remaining two guns continued in action until the last of the four hundred rounds had been fired. A few days later, when our infantry advanced over the sector this battery had shelled, the enemy's wire was found to have been completely cut.

So good was our counter-battery work that the enemy frequently withdrew his guns, and thus compelled us to postpone our attack in order that the new positions might be located. All through July our bombardment continued, till every corner of the Salient was drenched with our fire. We made constant raids and gas attacks, the latter with deadly effect; and it is worth noting that the place where the enemy seems to have suffered most from this weapon was precisely the region astride the Poelcapelle road, where in April 1915 he had made his first gas attack on the French and the Canadians. Towards the end of the month there were signs that von Armin might upset our plans by a withdrawal to his rear defences, and we had to keep jealous watch on the enemy's movements.

On 27th July, in the Boesinghe area, it was discovered that

his front trenches were unoccupied, and that he had fallen back some distance, whether out of fear of mines like those at Messines or from the sheer weight of our bombardment. Anthoine's right wing and Gough's left accordingly crossed the canal, and occupied the German front and support lines on a front of 3,000 yards. They held their ground till the attack began, and managed by night to throw seventeen bridges across the canal in their rear.

The front of attack was fifteen miles long, from the Lys River to a little north of Steenstraat, but the main effort was planned for the seven and a half miles between Boesinghe and the Zillebeke-Zandvoorde road. The Allied lines ran from the canal in a curve south-eastward through the village of Wieltje and along the foot of the low slope, which may be defined by the points Pilckem, Bellewaarde, Hooge, and Sanctuary Wood. Thence it ran south across the Ypres-Comines Canal to the Oosttaverne line, and thence to the Lys opposite La Basse Ville. It was the business of the French to clear the land between the canal and that mysterious creek which in its lower reaches is called the Martjevaart, and further up the St. Jansbeek. Their right had to cover much ground, for it had to keep pace with Gough's left.

The task of the British Fifth Army was, by a series of bounds, to capture the enemy's first defences situated on the forward slope of the rising ground, and his second position sited along the crest, and at the same time to secure the crossings of the Steenbeek or Hannebeek, the muddy ditch which flows by St. Julien to join the St. Jansbeek, north-east of Bixschoote. If this could be done at once and the weather favoured, a strong defensive flank could be formed for a break-through in the direction of Thourout towards the north-east. In the Fifth Army were four corps of assault—from left to right, the 14th, under Lord Cavan; the 18th, under Lieutenant-General Ivor Maxse; the 19th, under Lieutenant-General Watts; and the and, under Lieutenant-General Jacob.

The Second Army, on their right, had a strictly limited objective. Its right was ordered to take La Basse Ville, on the Lys, and its left to capture Hollebeke village, and clear the difficult ground north of the bend of the Ypres-Comines Canal and east of Battle Wood. Against the British attack alone the enemy had thirteen divisions in line, including the 3rd Guard Division, and four Bavarian—the 4th, 10th, 16th, and 6th Reserve.

The last week of July was dull, cloudy weather, with poor visibility for air work. On the morning of Monday, the 30th, came a heavy thunderstorm, and rain fell in the afternoon. All day the Allied bombardment continued at its height, and during the drizzling night. The rain stopped towards dawn, but a thick mist remained, and the ground was plashy and the skies overcast as zero hour drew near. There was a short lull in the firing after three; but precisely at 3.50 a.m. on the 31st the whole Allied front broke into flame. Under cover of discharges of thermit and blazing oil, and such a barrage as had not yet been seen, the infantry crossed their parapets, and the battle began.

The whole of the German front position fell at once. Anthoine crossed the canal and took Steenstraat. Verlorenhoek fell to the 15th Division, who that day added to a record of victories which included Martinpuich and Feuchy. Further south, pushing through Sanctuary Wood and Shrewsbury Forest, we carried the *château* of Hooge and the lake of Bellewaarde, and came to the foot of that lift of the Menin road which was the pillar of the enemy's position on the heights. The Allies then pressed on to the attack on the second position, and by nine in the morning the whole of it north of Westhoek was in their hands. Frezenberg, after a stubborn fight, was won by the 15th Division; English county troops entered St. Julien; and the 38th Welsh Division took Pilckem and annihilated the Fusilier regiment of the 3rd Prussian Guards. Pommern Redoubt, north of Frezenberg, was won by the 55th Division of West Lancashire Territorials. The 51st Highland Territorials and the Guards seized the crossings of the Steenbeek.

In a captured German document, which provided a "black list" of the British divisions, the 51st were given first place, and the enemy that day had no reason to revise his judgment. On the centre and left of our attack all our final objectives had been gained, and at one or two points we had gone beyond them. The French, for example, took Bixschoote; the Guards advanced beyond the Steenbeek; and at one point in our centre, we reached and penetrated the enemy's third trench system, that known as the Gheluvelt-Langemarck line.

More slow and difficult was the fighting on the right of the Fifth Army along the Menin road. Stirling Castle, the strong point which dominated Ypres south of the highway, was taken. But before the shell-shattered patches called Glencorse Wood and Inverness Copse the enemy had massed strongly for defence; for they were the key of his whole position, and the attacking brigades—Lancashire, Irish, and Scots—clung with difficulty to their footing on the ridge, but could go no further. In the afternoon, when a downpour of rain had begun to fall, the enemy counter-attacked from south of the Menin road to north of St. Julien. In spite of poor visibility owing to the thick weather, our artillery held him, though we had to fall back from all but the western skirts of Westhoek.

Our advanced troops north of St. Julien were also for the most part withdrawn to the line of the Steenbeek. By the evening the position was that everywhere we had carried the German first line, and had gained all the crest of the first ridge, and so denied the enemy observation over the Salient. From Westhoek to St. Julien we had taken the German second line, and north of St. Julien were well beyond it. On two-thirds of our front in the Salient we had won our first objectives, while, of the remaining third, we had just fallen short of our extreme aim on one-half, and on the other had exceeded it. On the whole battlefield we had taken over 6,000 prisoners, including 133 officers. It was no small triumph for an attack in foul weather over some of the most difficult country in which armies ever fought.

The subsidiary action fought by the Second Army was an unbroken success. On the right, after a fifty minutes' struggle, the New Zealand Division had carried La Basse Ville. Northward as far as Hollebeke we confined ourselves to advancing our front a few hundred yards to a line of strong points and fortified farms. On Plumer's left English county troops from the Midlands and the West pushed half a mile down the valley of the Roosebeek, and on one side of the Ypres-Comines Canal took the village of

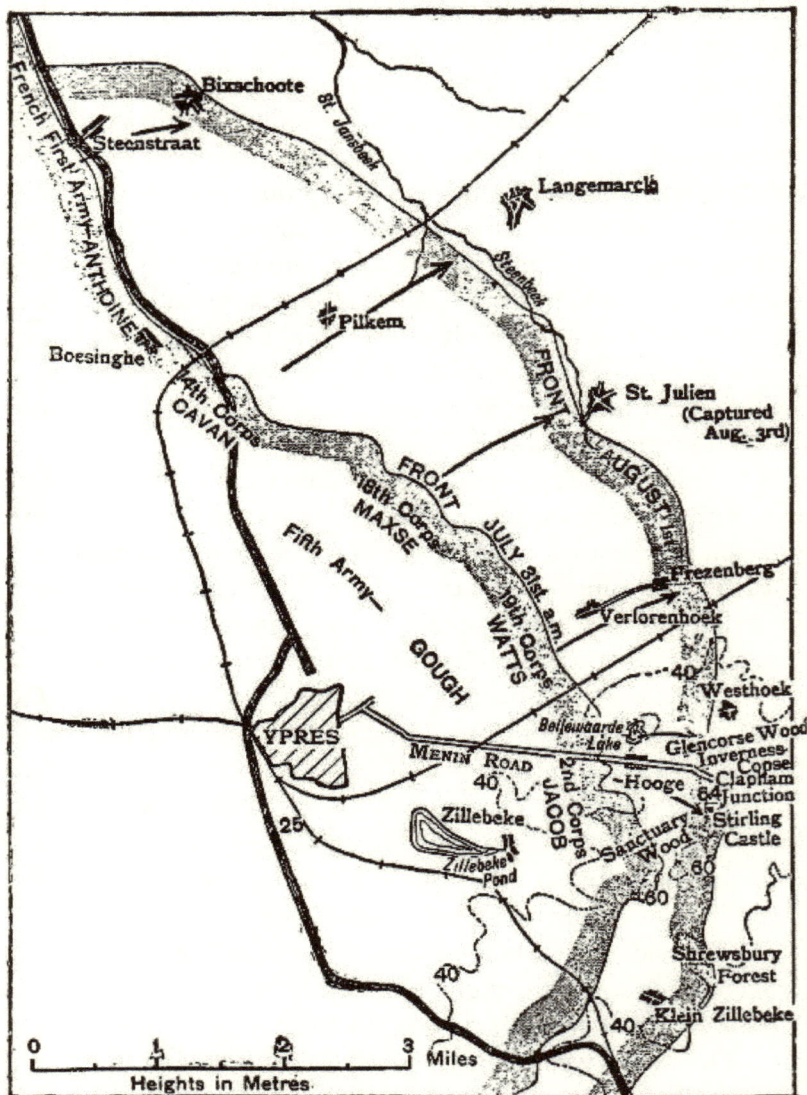

Advance of the First French and Fifth British Armies,
July 31, 1917.

Hollebeke, and on the other the rubble-heap which had been Klein Zillebeke. Once again after three years we held that classic soil where., at the close of a dark November day, Cavan's brigade of Guards and Kavanagh's dismounted Household Cavalry had turned the last wave of the German assault.

According to plan, the next day should have seen a second blow with cumulative force. But the weather had joined the enemy. From midday on 1st August for four days and four nights without intermission fell the rain. Even when it stopped on the 5th there followed days of sombre skies and wet mists and murky clouds. The misery of our troops, huddled in their impromptu lines or strung out in shell-holes, cannot be pictured in words. Nor can the supreme disappointment of the High Command. After months of thought and weeks of laborious preparation, just when a brilliant start had been made, they saw their hopes dashed to the ground. An offensive was still possible, but it could not be the offensive planned. The time-schedule was fatally dislocated. The situation is best described in the unemotional words of Sir Douglas Haig's dispatch:—

The low-lying, clayey soil, torn by shells and sodden by rain, turned to a succession of vast muddy pools. The valleys of the choked and overflowing streams were speedily transformed into long stretches of bog, impassable except by a few well-defined tracks, which became marks for the enemy's artillery. To leave these tracks was to risk death by drowning, and in the course of the subsequent fighting on several occasions both men and pack animals were lost in this way. In these conditions operations of any magnitude became impossible, and the resumption of our offensive was necessarily postponed until a period of fine weather should allow the ground to recover. As had been the case in the Arras battle, this unavoidable delay in the development of our offensive was of the greatest service to the enemy. Valuable time was lost, the troops opposed to us were able to recover from the disorganisation produced by our first attack, and the enemy was given the opportunity

133

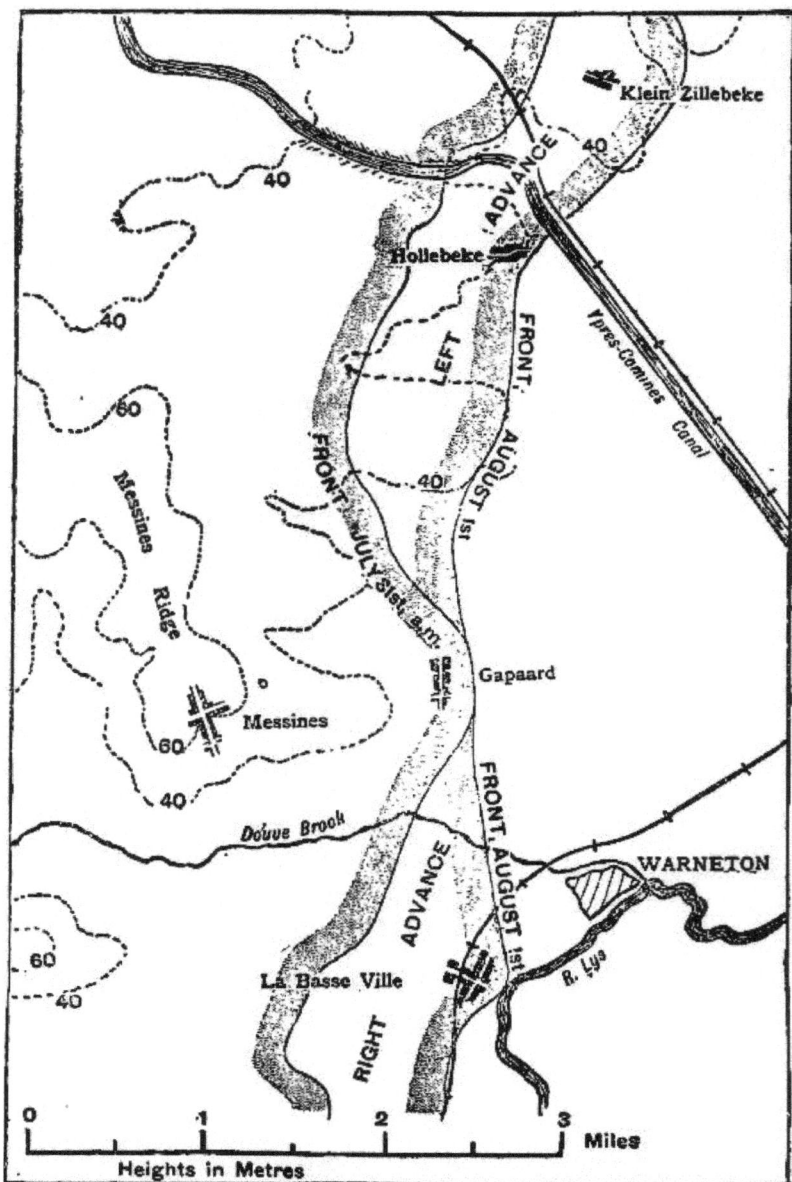

Sketch showing ground won by the Second Army on July 31st.

to bring up reinforcements.

For a fortnight we held our hand. To advance was a stark impossibility till the countryside was a little drier, for though we had won positions on the heights, our communications ran through the spongy Salient. The enemy's counter-attacks were to some extent also crippled by the weather. Those on the night of the first day of the battle were aimed at driving us off the high ground north of the Menin road, and regaining his second line system between Frezenberg and St. Julien. They failed to shake us; but it was considered wise, in order to escape the heavy shelling, to withdraw our men temporarily from St. Julien itself, though we still held a bridgehead on the Steenbeek, north of the village.

On 3rd August we reoccupied St. Julien, and consolidated our positions on the right bank of the Steenbeek by a line of points which linked us with the French. On 10th August we took the whole of Westhoek, and thereby won the last point in the old German second position which gave any chance of observation over Ypres. There the enemy counter-attacked violently and fruitlessly on the two following days. Meantime the French had cleared the ground around the Kortekeer Cabaret and its famous crossroads, and had forced their way well across the peninsula between the Yser Canal and the Martjevaart.

In the middle of the month there was a short break in the storms, and Sir Douglas Haig took advantage of it for a new attack. He began by a highly successful subsidiary action in the south, designed to threaten an important position of the enemy, and prevent him massing all his strength before the Salient. We have seen how, during the Battle of Arras and the lesser operations of July, the Canadian Corps had eaten into the defences of Lens from the south and south-west. The new attack came from the north-east, on a front of 4,000 yards, on a line south-east of Loos, running roughly from the Lens-Bethune road to the Bois Hugo. On September 15, 1915, at the Battle of Loos, troops of the 15th Division had swarmed across Hill 70 east of the village, and some had even penetrated into Cite St. Auguste, the mining suburb of Lens beyond the railway line. The latter never returned, and Hill 70, after a gallant defence against odds, was relinquished before the close of the battle.

Ever since then the place had been a thorn in our side, for it gave the enemy good observation. On 15th August, at 4.25 in the morning, the Canadians swept over Hill 70, and south of it crossed the Lens-La Bassée road, and took the *faubourgs* of Cité St. Laurent and Cité St. Emile. North of it they won the little Bois Rasé and the western half of the Bois Hugo. All their objectives were gained, except a short length of trench west of Cite St. Auguste, which fell the following afternoon. During the morning of the 15th counter-attacks by the German local reserves were easily beaten off, and in the evening a division of the German Guard was thrown in without better success. They were caught in the open by the deadly rifle and machine-gun fire of the Canadians. From the three German divisions opposed to us that day we took 1,120 prisoners.

Next day, the 16th, saw the second stage of the Ypres struggle. The Fifth Army was directed against the German third position, the Gheluvelt-Langemarck line, which ran from the Menin road along the second of the tiers of ridges which rimmed the Salient on the east. These tiers, the highest and most easterly of which was the famous Passchendaele crest, had the common features that they all sprang from one southern boss or pillar, the point on the Menin road marked 64 metres, which we knew as Clapham Junction, and all as they ran northward lost elevation. The day was destined to show at its best von Armin's new defensive methods. The weather was still thick and damp, making aeroplane observation difficult, and therefore depriving us of timely notice of the enemy's counter-attacks. His front was sown with "pillboxes," the tactical device which as yet we scarcely understood, and had not found a weapon to meet. The ground was sloppy, and made tangled and difficult with broken woods.

The conditions were ideal for the practice of that method which von Armin had foreshadowed at Messines and had now definitely embraced—that system of "elastic defence," in the words of the official dispatch:

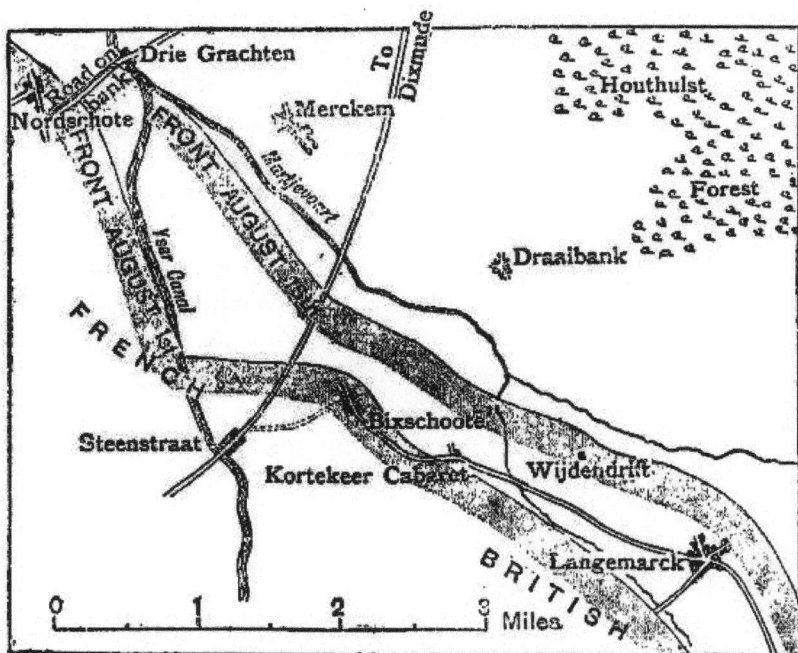

Gains on the Allied Left in the attack on August 16, 1917.

In which his forward trench lines were held only in sufficient strength to disorganise the attack, while the bulk of his forces were kept in close reserve, ready to deliver a powerful and immediate blow which might recover the positions overrun by our troops before we had had time to consolidate them.

The attack took place at dawn, 4.45 a.m., and on the Allies' left and left centre had an immediate success. The French cleared the whole peninsula between the Yser Canal and the Martjevaart, and, wading through deep floods, captured the strongly fortified bridgehead of Drie Grachten. The British left pressed on beyond the Bixschoote-Langemarck road, and took the hamlet of Wijdendrift. At first, they were checked in the outskirts of Langemarck; but by eight o'clock they held the village, and by nine they had won their final objective, the portion of the German third line system half a mile farther north.

Very different was the fate of the British centre. North and north-east of St. Julien, and between the Wieltje-Passenchdaele and the Ypres-Zonnebeke roads, they came up against the full strength of the "pill-boxes." A number fell to us, and all day we struggled on in the mud, losing heavily from the concealed machine-gun fire. In some places our men reached their final objectives, but they could not abide in them. Enemy counter-attacks later in the morning forced us back, and at the close of the day we were little beyond our starting-point. Our Langemarck gains were, however, secured, for the 55th West Lancashire Territorial Division had established a defensive flank on a line from east of Langemarck to north of St. Julien.

On the British right the fighting was still more desperate. On the Menin road we had already passed the highest point, Hill 64, and were moving on the wood of Herenthage, which we called Inverness Copse, and which lay on the slopes towards Gheluvelt. This wood was intersected by the highway, and north of it lay the Nuns' Wood, with its southern outlier, which we knew as Glencorse Wood. East of Glencorse Wood was the big Polygon Wood, with the remains of a racecourse in the heart of it. In all this area our advance was most stubbornly contested, and at the end of the day we had done no more than gain a fraction of the western edge of Glencorse Wood, and advance a little way north of Westhoek. Taking the battleground as a whole, as a result of the day we had made a considerable gap in the German third line, and taken over two thousand prisoners and thirty guns.

The rest of the month was one long downpour. We made a few small gains—notably on the 19th, 22nd, and 27th, when, with the assistance of tanks, we improved our position on a two-mile front between St. Julien and the Ypres-Roulers railway, and took a number of strong points and fortified farms. On the 22nd we also attacked along the Menin road, and after six days' continuous fighting made some way in Glencorse Wood, and won the western edge of Inverness Copse.

This second stage of the battle was beyond doubt a serious British check. We had encountered a new tactical device of the enemy, and it had defeated us. The Fifth Army had fought with the most splendid gallantry, but their courage had been largely fruitless. We had no doubt caused the enemy serious losses, but he had taken a heavier toll of our own ranks. Fine brigades had been hurled in succession against a concrete wall, and had been sorely battered. For almost the first time in the campaign there was a sense of discouragement abroad on our front. Men felt that they were being sacrificed blindly; that every fight was a soldiers' fight, and that such sledge-hammer tactics were too crude to meet the problem. For a moment there was a real ebb of confidence in British leadership. That such a feeling should exist among journalists and politicians matters nothing; but it matters much if it is found among troops in the field.

Sir Douglas Haig accordingly brought upon the scene the man who was rapidly coming to recognition as the most re-sourceful of army commanders. The front of the Second Army was extended northward, and Sir Herbert Plumer took over the attack upon the southern portion of the enemy front on the Menin road. The better part of a month was spent in preparation, while Plumer patiently thought out the problem. Sorely tried—too sorely tried—divisions were taken out of the line to rest, and the dispositions on the whole front of assault were readjusted. Especially our artillery tactics were revised, in order to cope with the "pill-boxes." In the early days of September, the weather improved, and the sodden Salient began slowly to dry. That is to say, the mud hardened into something like the *seracs* of a glacier, and the streams became streams again, and not lagoons. But the process was slow, and it was not till the third week of the month that the next stage in the battle could begin.

The new eight-mile front of attack ran from the Ypres-Staden railway north of Langemarck to the Ypres-Comines Canal north of Hollebeke. On the left and centre our objectives were narrowly limited, averaging about three-quarters of a mile; but Plumer on the right had the serious task of pushing for a mile along the Menin road. The "pill-box" problem had been studied, and a solution, it was believed, had been found, not by miraculous ingenuity, but by patience and meticulous care. The little fortalices had been methodically reconnoitred, and our heavy barrage so arranged as to cover each mark.

Even when a direct hit was not attained, it was believed that the concussion of the great shells might loosen some of the lesser structures, while fumes, smoke, and gas would make the life of the inmates difficult. One famous division followed with complete success another plan. Having located the "pill-box," the field-gun barrage lengthened on both sides of it; which enabled the advancing troops, hugging their barrage, to get round its unprotected rear.

Wednesday, 19th September, was a clear blowing day, but at nine o'clock in the evening the rain began, and fell heavily all that night.

At dawn the drizzle stopped, but a wet mist remained, which blinded our air reconnaissance.

At 5.40 a.m. on the 20th the attack was launched. Presently the fog cleared, and the sun came out, and our aeroplanes were able to fight in line with the infantry, attacking enemy trenches and concentrations with machine-gun fire. The ground was knee-deep in mud, but the whole British line pressed forward. The Fifth Army's left north of the Zonnebeke-Langemarck road—the 47th London Division and the 51st Highland Territorials—won all its objectives by midday. South of them the 55th West Lancashire Territorials were not less successful in the appalling mud south-east of St. Julien. Perhaps the most remarkable achievement was that of the Scottish and South African brigades of the 9th Division, which, advancing on both sides of the Ypres-Roulers railway, won their final objectives in three hours. They carried a line of fortified farms, the two important redoubts called Zonnebeke and Bremen, and the hamlet of Zevenkote.

But the crux of the battle lay in the area of the Second Army, and the vital point was the work of its centre along the Menin road. There lay the key of the enemy's position, and there in defence he had already sent in sixteen divisions. That day the fighting was extended well south of the highroad. Plumer's right—Welsh and West of England troops—cleared the small woods north of the Ypres-Comines Canal. Farther north they pushed through the eastern fringe of Shrewsbury Forest, across the stream called the Bassevillebeek, which drains to the Lys, with its hideous cluster of ponds called Dumbarton Lakes, and up the slopes of the Tower Hamlets spur, on the eastern side of which lay Gheluvelt.

Here they encountered heavy machinegun fire from the ridge between Veldhoek and the Tower Hamlets. On the left the 23rd Division of English north-country troops had been brilliantly successful. They had carried the whole of Inverness Copse, and had captured Veldhoek itself, as a result of which late in the day we were able to establish ourselves across the Tower Hamlets spur.

The Australians, on Plumer's left, had for their first task the clearing of the rest of Glencorse Wood and the Nuns' Wood. This they achieved early in the morning, and by 10 a.m. had taken Polygon veld, at the north-western corner of the great Polygon Wood. For a little they were held up at Black Watch Corner, at the south-western angle; but by midday they had passed it, and had secured the whole western half of the wood up to the racecourse, thus reaching their final objectives.

This day's battle cracked the kernel of the German defence in

The British Advance, September 20, 1917.

the Salient. It showed a limited advance, and the total of 3,000 prisoners had been often exceeded in a day's fighting; but every inch of the ground won was vital. We had carried the southern pillar on which the security of the Passchendaele ridge depended. Few struggles in the campaign were more desperate, or carried out on a more gruesome battlefield. The maze of quagmires, splintered woods, ruined husks of "pillboxes," water-filled shell-holes, and foul creeks which made up the land on both sides of the Menin road was a sight which to the recollection of most men must seem like a fevered nightmare.

It was the classic soil on which during the First Battle of Ypres the 1st and 2nd Divisions had stayed the German rush for the Channel. Then it had been a broken but still recognisable and featured countryside; now the elements seemed to have blended with each other to make of it a limbo outside mortal experience and almost beyond human imagining. Only on some of the tortured hills of Verdun could a parallel be found. The battle of 20th September was a proof of what heights of endurance the British soldier may attain to. It was an example, too, of how thought and patience may achieve success in spite of every disadvantage of weather, terrain, and enemy strength.

Von Armin could not accept meekly the losses of the 20th. That afternoon and evening he made no less than eleven counter-attacks. Most of them failed, but east of St. Julien he retook a farm which we did not win back till the next day. North-east of Langemarck a short length of German trench held out till the 23rd. On the 21st, and for the four days following, he attacked north-east of St. Julien, and very fiercely on the front between the Tower Hamlets and the Polygon Wood. On the 25th the Germans got into our lines north of the Menin road; but after a struggle of many hours, British and Australian troops succeeded in ejecting them. In the meantime, preparations were being hastened on for the next stage.

We had now won all the interior ridges of the Salient and the southern pillar; but we were not yet within striking distance of the north part of the main Passchendaele ridge. To attain this, we must lie east of Zonnebeke and the Polygon Wood at the foot

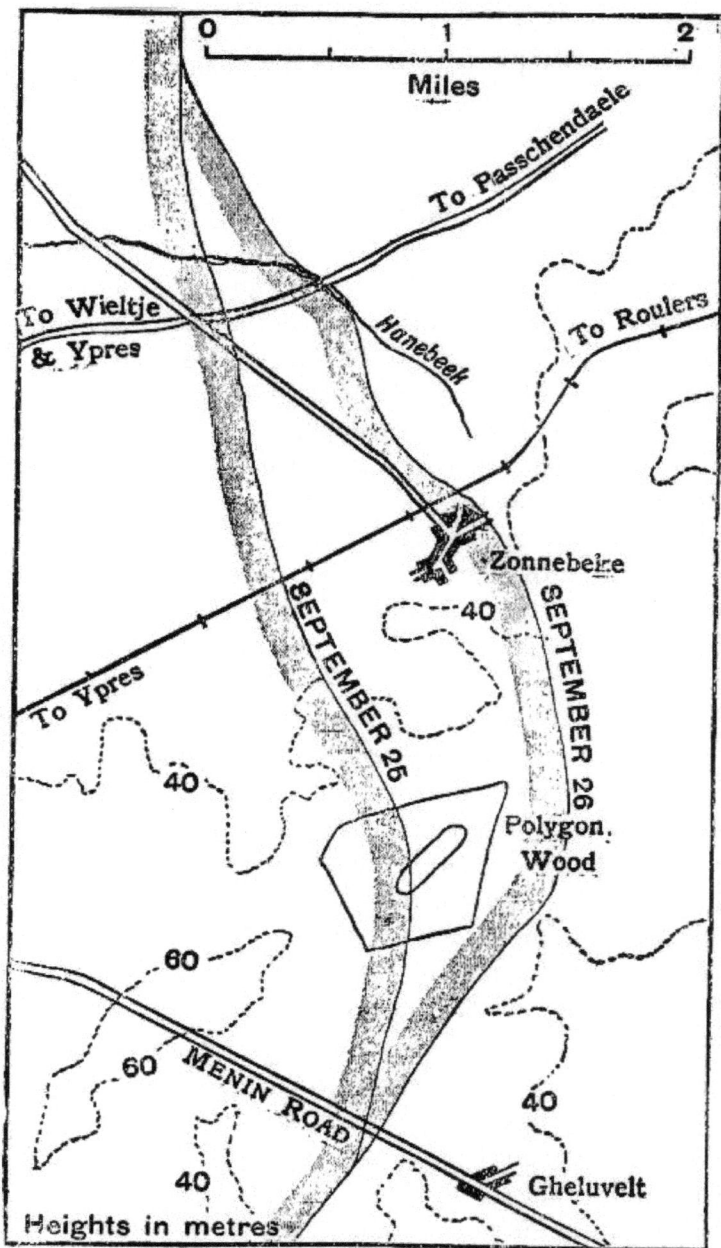

The British Advance, September 26, 1917.

of the final slopes. Moreover, we must act quickly. We were well aware that the enemy intended a counter-attack in force, and it was our object to anticipate him.

We struck again on 26th September. The weather was fine, and for a brief week it ceased to be an element in the German defensive. Our front of attack was the six-mile stretch from north-east of St. Julien to south of the Tower Hamlets. The new advance was as precise and complete as its predecessor of the 20th. At ten minutes to six our infantry moved forward. On our left the North Midlanders and a London Territorial division pushed on both sides of the Wieltje-Passchendaele road to the upper course of the Haanebeek. In the centre, after some sharp fighting along the Ypres-Roulers railway line, we took the ruins of Zonnebeke village—which had been the apex of the Salient when we evacuated it in May 1915.

Further south the Australians carried the remainder of the Polygon Wood; while they also assisted the sorely tried British division on their right, which was struggling in the maze of creeks and trenches beyond Veldhoek. This division, though it had suffered one of the enemy's severest counterstrokes the day before, nevertheless was able to join in the general advance. One dramatic performance fell to its share. It was able to relieve two companies of Argyll and Sutherland Highlanders, who had been isolated the night before, and had held out for twelve hours in the midst of the enemy.

The last days of fine weather were employed by the Germans in some of the most resolute counter-attacks of the battle. The troops which they had intended to use in their frustrated offensive of the 26th were now employed to undo the effects of our advance. There were seven attacks during the day, notably in the area between the Reutelbeek and the Polygon Wood. Then came a pause, while he collected his shattered strength; and on the last day of the month, he began again with two *flammenwerfer* attacks north of the Menin road. Five more followed next day in the same place, and one south of the Roulers railway. Nothing came of them, except the temporary loss of two advanced posts south-east of the Polygon Wood. The last took place on 3rd October, close to the Menin road, but it was broken up by our guns before it reached our lines.

That night the weather broke, and a gale from the south-west brought heavy rains. It was the old ill-luck of our army, for on the 4th we had planned the next stage of the battle. But if the weather was ill-timed, not so was our attack. The enemy had brought up three fresh divisions, with a view to recovering his losses of the 26th. Ten minutes past six was his zero hour, and by good fortune and good guiding six o'clock was ours. Our barrage burst upon his infantry when it was forming up for the assault, and cut great swathes in its ranks. While the Germans were yet in the confusion of miscarried plans our bayonets were upon them.

Our objective was the line of the main ridge east of Zonnebeke, the southern part of what was called the Passchendaele heights, along which ran the north road from Becelaere. Our main front was the seven miles from the Ypres-Staden railway to the Menin road, though we also advanced a short distance south of that highway. By midday every objective had been gained. The achievement of Messines and the first day of Arras was repeated. The enemy, caught on the brink of an attack of his own, was not merely repulsed; a considerable part of his forces was destroyed.

The British left was directed along the Poelcapelle road, in a country so nearly flat that the chief feature was a hill marked 19 metres. After a sharp struggle we won this position, lost it, and regained it before evening. Further south we entered Poelcapelle village, and occupied its western half. The valley of the Stroombeek was a sea of mud, but the South Midland Division forced their way across it. In our centre lay the area of the projected German attack—the Gravenstafel ridge jutting west from the Passchendaele heights, and the central part of the heights themselves. The New Zealand Division, struggling across the swamps of the Upper Haanebeek, took the village of Gravenstafel and won the crest of the spur.

On their right, the Australians carried Molenaarelsthoek and Broodseinde, and drove the 4th Prussian Guards from the ridge summit, pressing beyond the Becelaire-Passchendaele road. Southward, again, British troops traversed the crest and took Noordemdhoek, while the division on their right took the village of Reutel and cleared the tangled ground east of the Polygon Wood. Thence as far as the Menin road there was desperate fighting in the hollows of the Reutelbeek and the Polygonbeek, where men of South England and the Scottish Borders stormed the Polderhoek Château.

A little after midday we had gained all our final objectives. We had broken up forty German battalions, and had taken over 5,000 prisoners, including 138 officers. The counter-attacks which followed—there were no less than eight between the Menin road and Reutel—won back little ground. From Mount Sorrel, in the south, we held 9,000 yards of the crest of the ultimate ridge, and our grip of the Gravenstafel spur gave us a good defensive flank on the north. Above all, we had succeeded in nullifying von Armin's tactics of defence; and we captured documents which made it plain that the German High Command were wavering, and inclined to a return to their old method of holding their front line in force. Sir Herbert Plumer's leadership had been abundantly justified.

But October had set in, storm followed storm, and Sir Douglas Haig had to reconsider his plan of campaign. Weather and a dozen other malignant accidents had wrecked the larger scheme of a Flanders offensive. Gone was the hope of clearing the coast or of driving the enemy out of his Flemish bases. What had been laboriously achieved at the end of ten weeks had been in the programme for the first fortnight. It was only a preliminary; the main objectives lay beyond the Passchendaele ridge. The weather had compelled us to make our advance by stages, widely separated in time, with the result that the enemy had been able to bring up his reserves and reorganise his defence. Our pressure could not be cumulative, and we had been unable to reap the full fruits of each success.

There was, therefore, no chance of any decisive operation in the Flanders area. The success of Cadorna on the Bainsizza plateau, which we shall consider later, had unsettled the minds

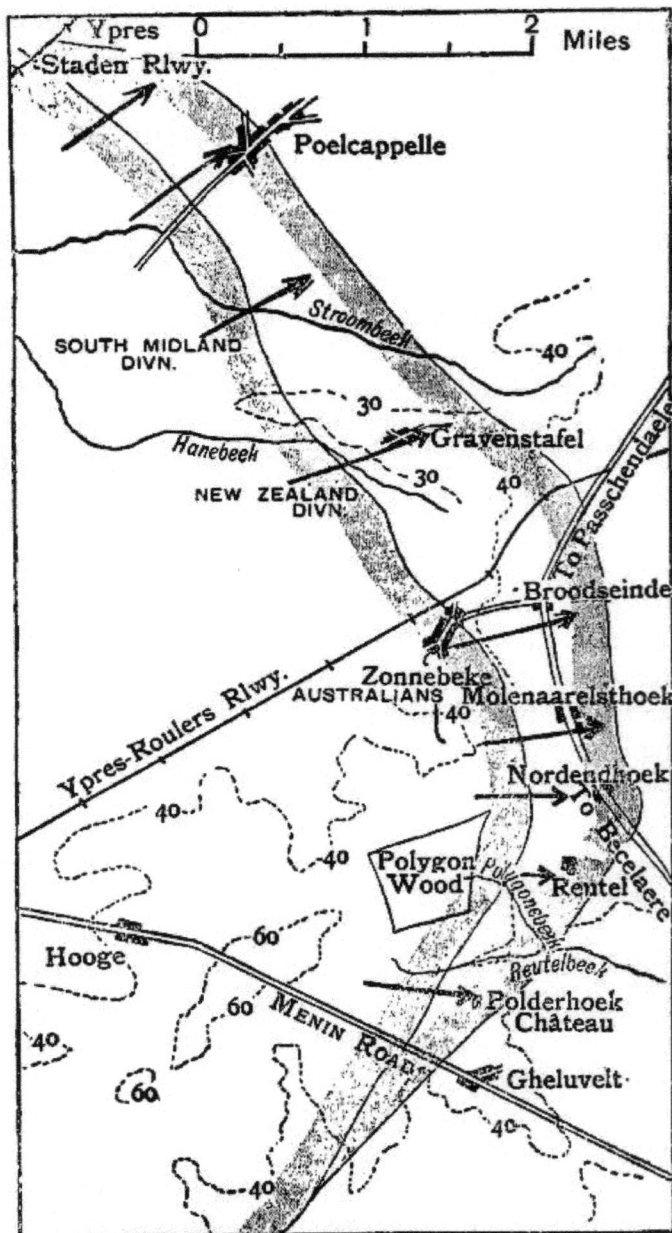

The British Advance, October 4, 1917.

of certain civilian statesmen, and given rise to a scheme, mooted about this time, for sending British and French reserves to the Isonzo front, in the hope of striking a final blow at Austria. This highly divergent operation was, fortunately, rejected; but it was a serious question for Sir Douglas Haig whether the Ypres operations should be continued. If October should show the kind of weather which it had yielded the year before on the Somme, the Salient would be an ugly fighting ground.

The extremity of Russia was permitting more and more German divisions to be transferred to the West; which would not make our task easier. On the other hand, we had not won the last even of the limited preliminary objectives; for we did not control the whole Passchendaele ridge, and it might well be urged that, till we did, we had not secured our own position or made difficult the enemy's against the coming winter. Moreover, the French were preparing a great attack on the Aisne heights for the last week of the month, and it was desirable that the German mind should be kept engrossed with the northern front. Balancing the pros and cons of the matter, Sir Douglas Haig resolved to continue his offensive till the end of October, or such time as would give our men the chance of reaching Passchendaele.

The last stages of the Third Battle of Ypres were probably the muddiest combats ever known in the history of war. It rained incessantly—sometimes clearing to a drizzle or a Scots mist, but relapsing into a downpour on any day fixed for our attack. The British movements became an accurate barometer: whenever it was more than usually tempestuous it was safe to assume that some zero hour was near. Tuesday, the 9th, was the day fixed for an advance on a broad front by both French and British; but all day on the 7th and 8th it rained, and the night of the 8th was black darkness above and a melting earth beneath. It was a difficult task assembling troops under such conditions; but the thing was accomplished, and at twenty minutes past five in the dripping dawn of the 9th our infantry moved forward.

The operations of the 4th had bulged our centre between Poelcapelle and Becelaere, and it was necessary to bring up our

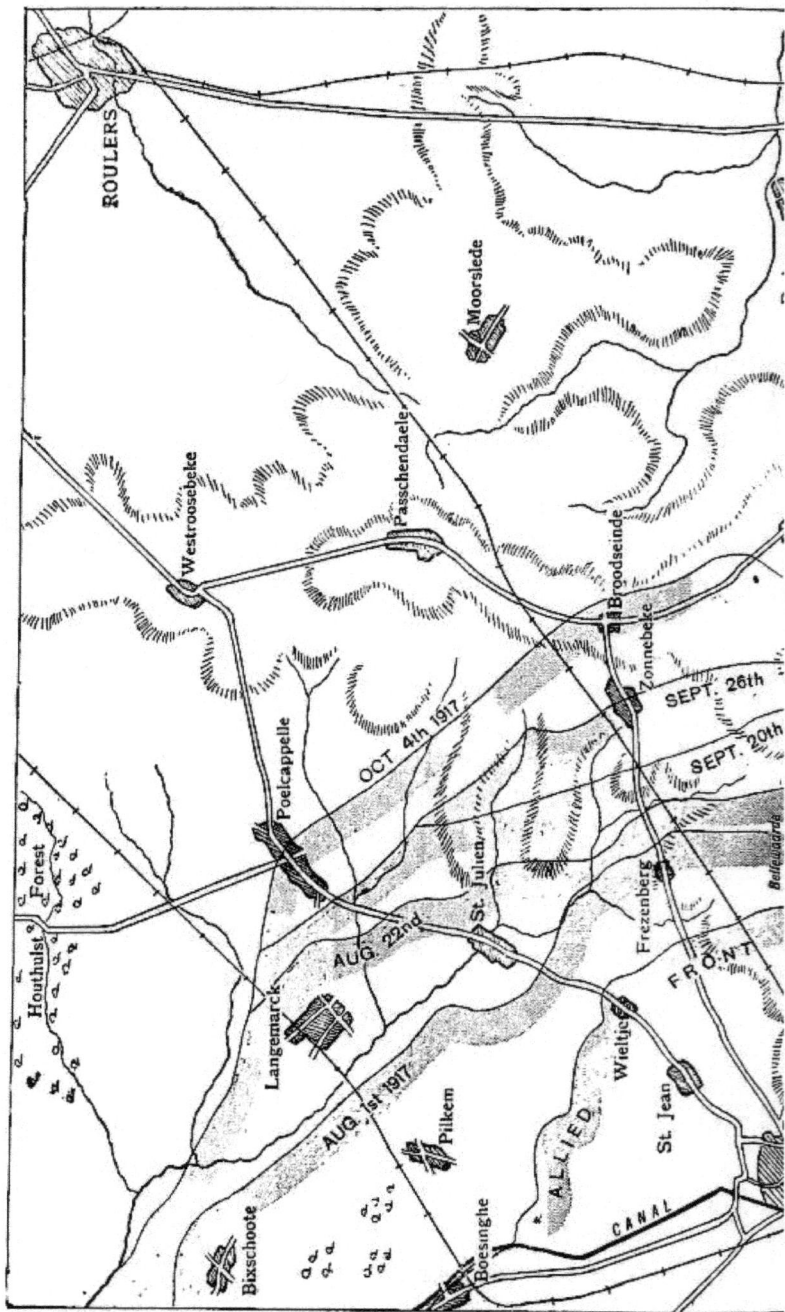

ROULERS

Moorslede

Westroosebeke

Passchendaele

Broodseinde

Zonnebeke

SEPT. 26th

OCT 4th 1917

SEPT. 20th

Poelcappelle

Houthulst Forest

St. Julien

Frezenberg

Bellewaarde

AUG. 22nd

FRONT

Langemarck

Wieltje

Pilkem

ALLIED

St. Jean

AUG. 1st 1917

Bixschoote

Boesinghe

CANAL

The country between the Ypres Salient and the Roulers-Menin Line, showing the progress of the Offensive up to the first week of October 1917.

left wing. Hence, though we attacked everywhere from the Polygon Wood northward, our main effort was on the six miles from a point east of Zonnebeke to the north-west of Langemarck; while the French, on our left, continued the front of assault to the edge of the St. Jansbeek, south of Draaibank.

In the north the French and the British Guards Division, advancing side by side, had won all their objectives by the early afternoon. They crossed the St. Jansbeek, carried the hamlets of St. Janshoek, Mangelaare, Veldhoek, and Koekuit, and established themselves on the skirts of the great Houthulst Forest, the northern pillar of the German line. South of the Ypres-Staden railway English divisions fought their way east of the Poelcapelle-Houthulst road, and captured the whole of the ruins of Poelcapelle. In the centre the Australians and British Territorial troops—the latter from Yorkshire, Lancashire, and the Southern Midlands—moved nearer to Passchendaele along the main ridge, taking the hamlets of Nieuwemolen and Keerselaarhoek. The day was successful, for our final objectives were almost everywhere attained, and over 2,000 prisoners were taken.

It was Sir Douglas Haig's intention to press on the advance, for the weather and the landscape were such that there was less hardship in going on than in staying still in lagoons and shell-craters, where comfort or security was unattainable. The next attack was fixed for Friday, the 12th; but the rain fell in sheets during the night of the 11th, and the movement was countermanded soon after it had begun. Nevertheless, we made some progress between the Roulers railway and Houthulst Forest, and 1,000 prisoners were taken. Such fighting was the last word in human misery, for the country was now one irreclaimable bog, and the occasional hours of watery sunshine had no power to dry it.

"You might as well," wrote one correspondent, "try to empty a bath by holding lighted matches over it." But Sir Douglas Haig still kept his eye on Passchendaele, and, moreover, he was maturing another plan of operations far in the south, which made it imperative to sustain the northern pressure for a week or two. Also, there was the French attack on the Aisne heights now drawing very near. So, the battle among the shell-holes and

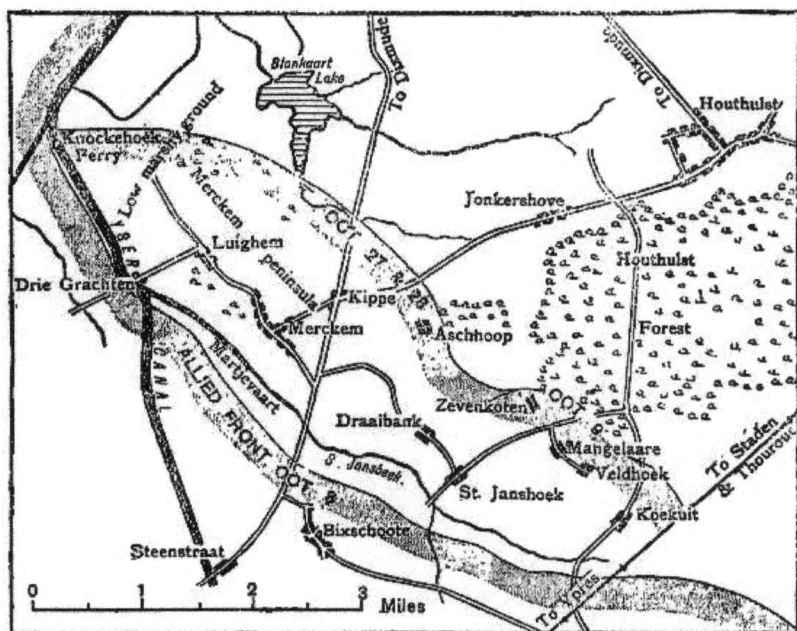

Ground gained on the Allied Left in October.

swamps still continued.

On the 22nd we pushed east of Poelcapelle, and crept a little farther into the Houthulst Wood. On the 25th we had a stroke of fortune, for a strong wind blew from the west which slightly hardened the ground. On the 26th the rain returned, but at a quarter to six in the morning we attacked on a front from the Roulers railway to beyond Poelcapelle. From Passchendaele the Bellevue spur runs westward, and between it and the Gravenstafel spur is the valley of a brooklet called the Ravebeek, a tributary of the Stroombeek. Along this stream the Canadian troops moved against the main ridge, and won the little hill just south of Passchendaele village. Their left had a hard struggle on the Bellevue spur, where the old main Staden-Zonnebeke line of the German defences ran; but the place was carried in the afternoon at the second attempt, and by the evening the Canadians held all their objectives.

On the left of the Canadians the 63rd (Royal Naval) Division and a division of London Territorials continued the advance in the low-lying ground north of the Bellevue ridge. That day on our right British troops entered Gheluvelt for the first time since the First Battle of Ypres. Their rifles, however, were choked with mud, and they were compelled to withdraw before the enemy's counter-attack.

On that day, the 26th, the French on our left were busy bridging the St. Jansbeek, in its lower course west of Draaibank. Their object was to clear the ground called the Merckem peninsula, between the Blankaart Lake, the Martjevaart or St. Jansbeek, and the Yser Canal. On the 27th they were in action along with the Belgians on their left, who crossed the Yser at Knockehoek. The Allies won the villages of Aschhoop, Kippe, and Merckem, and reached the southern shore of the Blankaart Lake. By the morning of the 28th the whole of the Merckem peninsula had been cleared of the enemy. This success menaced from the west the Forest of Houthulst.

On 30th October came the attack on Passchendaele itself. At 5.50 a.m., in a clear, cold dawn, the Canadians attacked from the top of the Ravebeek valley and along the crest of the ridge, while the London Territorials and the Royal Naval Division moved up the Paddebeek rivulet which runs north of the Bellevue spur. At ten in the morning the rain began again, and the strength of the enemy position, and the desperate resistance of the 5th and 11th Bavarian Divisions which held it, made the day one of the severest in the battle. The Canadians won Crest Farm, south of the village, and carried also the spur west of the village, and held it against five counter-attacks. They forced their way into the outskirts of Passchendaele; but the appalling condition of the Paddebeek valley prevented the Londoners and the Royal Naval Division from advancing far, so that the Canadian front formed a sharp salient.

But the end was not far off. Some days of dry weather followed, during which small advances were made to improve our position. At 6 a.m. on Tuesday, 6th November, the Canadians swept forward again, carried the whole of Passchendaele, and pushed northward to the Goudberg spur. Four days later they increased their gains, so that all the vital part of the main ridge of West Flanders was in British hands. We dominated the enemy's hinterland in the flats towards Roulers and Thourout, and he had the prospect of a restless winter under our direct observation. The Third Battle of Ypres had wiped out the Salient where for three years we had been at the mercy of the German guns.

The great struggle which we have described was strategically a British failure. We did not come within measurable distance of our major purpose, and that owing to no fault of generalship or fighting virtue, but through the maleficence of the weather in a terrain where weather was all in all. We gambled upon a normal August, and we did not get it. The sea of mud which lapped around the Salient was the true defence of the enemy. Consequently, the battle, which might have had a profound strategic significance in the campaign, became merely an episode in the war of attrition, a repetition of the Somme tactics, though conspicuously less successful and considerably more costly than the fighting of 1916.

Since 31st July we had taken 24,065 prisoners, 74 guns, 941 machine guns, and 138 trench mortars. We had drawn in seven-

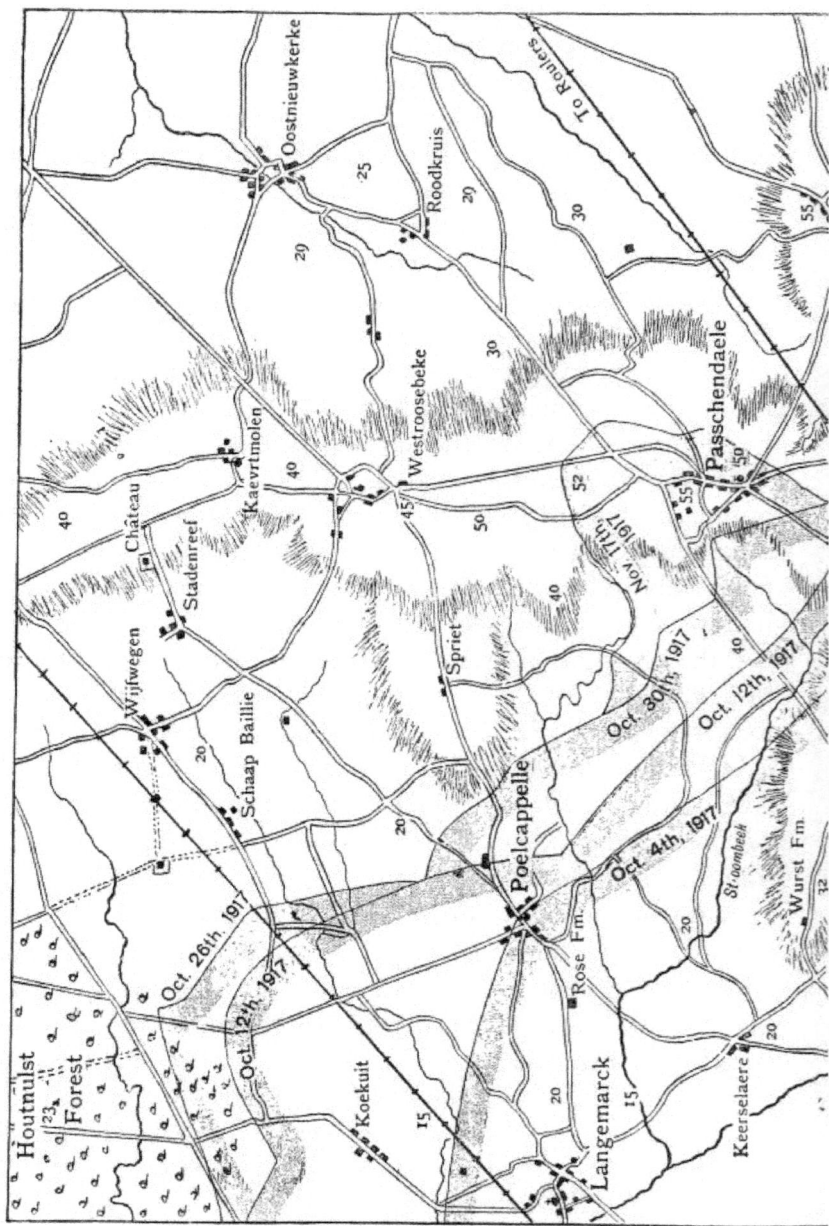

Houtnulst Forest

Oostnieuwkerke

Roodkruis

Passchendaele

To Roulers

Westroosebeke

Kaevrtmolen

Château

Stadenreef

Wijfwegen

Schaap Baillie

Spriet

Nov. 11th 1917

Oct. 30th, 1917

Oct. 12th, 1917

Oct. 4th, 1917

Oct. 26th. 1917

Oct. 12th, 1917

Poelcappelle

Rose Fm.

Wurst Fm.

St.-oombeek

Koekuit

Langemarck

Keerselaere

25

20

29

30

30

40

45

50

52

55

50

55

40

40

40

20

20

20

15

15

20

15

20

20

40

22

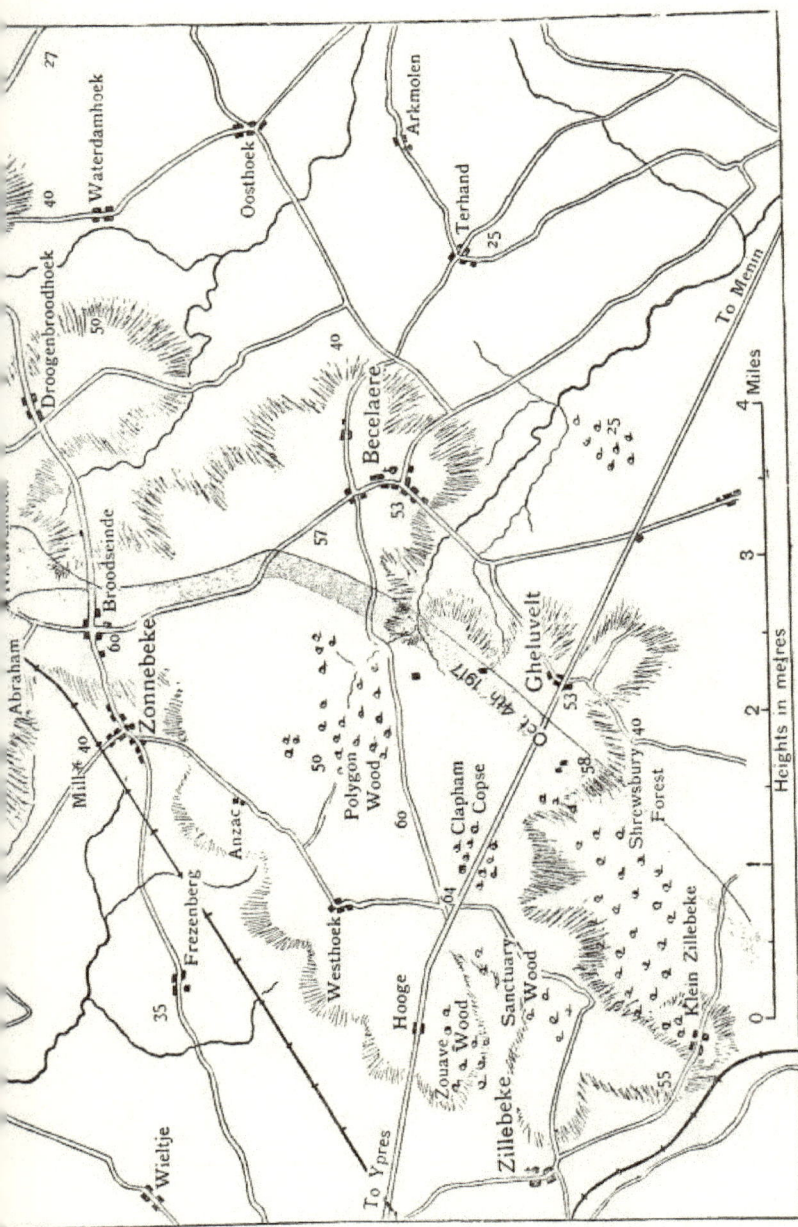

The Passchendaele Ridge.

Waterdamhoek
Arkmolen
Oosthoek
Terhand
27
40
25
To Menn
Droogenbroodhoek
50
Becelaere
40
25
57
53
Broodseinde
60
Cheluvelt
53
Abraham
Zonnebeke
Oct. 4th 1917
Mill 40
58
Shrewsbury 40
Polygon
Wood
50
Clapham
Copse
60
Forest
Frezenberg
Anzac
35
Westhoek
64
Sanctuary
Wood
Klein Zillebeke
Wieltje
Hooge
Zouave
Wood
Zillebeke
55
To Ypres

Heights in metres

0   1   2   3   4 Miles

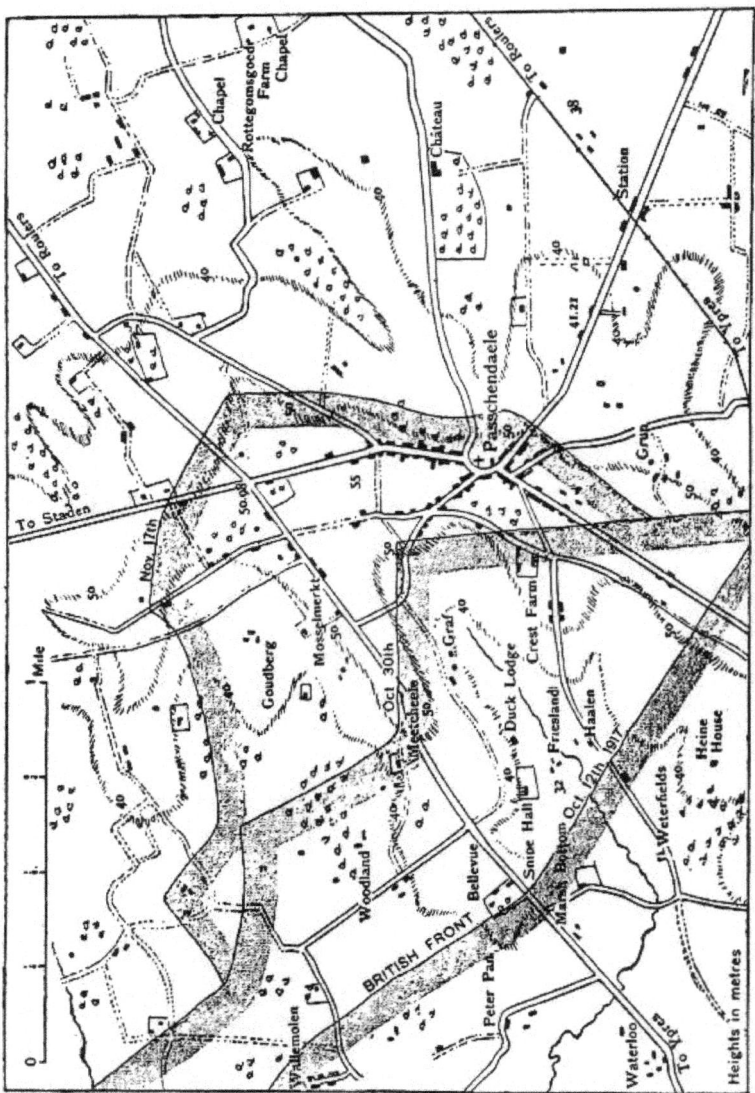

Passschendaele.

ty-eight German divisions, of which eighteen had been engaged a second or a third time. But, to set against this, our own losses had been severe, and the enemy had now a big reservoir for re-inforcements. Already forty fresh divisions had been transferred to the West from the Russian front, apart from drafts of men to replace losses in other units.

The outstanding fact of the battle was the superb endurance and valour of the new armies of Britain, fighting under condi-tions which for horror and misery had scarcely been paralleled in war. To them the commander-in-chief paid a worthy trib-ute:—

Throughout the northern operations our troops have been fighting over ground every foot of which is sacred to the memory of those who, in the First and Second Battles of Ypres, fought and died to make possible the victories of the armies which today are rolling back the tide stayed by their sacrifices. It is no disparagement of the gallant deeds performed on other fronts to say that, in the stub-born struggle for the line of hills which stretches from Wytschaete to Passchendaele, the great armies that today are shouldering the burden of our Empire have shown themselves worthy of the regiments which, in October and November of 1914, made Ypres take rank for ever amongst the most glorious of British battles.

Ypres was to Britain what Verdun was to France—the hal-lowed soil which called forth the highest virtue of her people. It was a battleground where there could be no failure without loss of honour. The armies which fought there in the autumn of 1917 were very different from the few divisions which had held the fort during the earlier struggles. But there were links of con-nection. The Guards, by more than one resistless advance, were recompensed for the awful tension of October 1914, when at Gheluvelt and Klein Zillebeke some of their best battalions had been destroyed. And it fell to Canada, by the crowning victory at Passchendaele, to avenge the gas attack of April 1915, when only her dauntless two brigades stood between Ypres and the enemy.

The battlefield of the old Salient was now as featureless as the Sahara or the mid-Atlantic. All landmarks had been obliterated; the very ridges and streams had changed their character. The names which still crowded the map had no longer any geographical counterpart. They were no more than measurements on a plane, as abstract as the points of the mathematician. It was war bared to the buff, stripped of any of the tattered romance which has clung to older fields. And yet in its very grossness it was war sublimated, for the material appanages had vanished. The quaint Flemish names belonged not now to the solid homely earth; they seemed rather points on a spiritual map, marking advance and retreat in the gigantic striving of the souls of peoples.

Tim Harington Looks Back (Extract)

By Sir Charles Harington

WAR OFFICE & ALDERSHOT

In the spring of 1908, I went to the War Office as an attached officer and, in 1909, became a G.S.O.3 in the Staff Duties Branch and was employed in dealing with Promotion Examinations. In those days we lived at Eastcote, near Pinner, and I used to go up by train daily. My particular work was to get suitable examiners, and to check and work out their questions before they were set to the candidates. Although, quite naturally, when in that branch one could not be an examiner, yet in later years they were very kind to me, and up to the start of the Great War I really lived by examination work.

Actually, during the Retreat from Mons, I received a cheque for having set and corrected a Strategy Paper for the Staff College just before the war. I used to set papers for Sandhurst and Woolwich, Promotion, Staff College, etc., but the best and most profitable used to be the 1st Class Certificate Examination for N.C.O.s in Map Reading. The answers were all shown on a map. With a correct map before one it was easy to see at a glance how a candidate had fared, and as one threw down each map on the floor it meant a shilling. The first time I took on that examination there were 1,087 candidates!

Whilst I was at the War Office, King Edward VII died, and I was appointed a marshalling officer at his funeral. I had to marshal his late household. I shall never forget it. As soon as ever I got four of them into position in a section of fours, one would

Sir Charles Harington

spot an old friend miles away and rush off to talk to him. I shall always remember that march to Westminster Abbey and thence to Paddington. Just as the Q. M.G., General Sir Herbert Miles in full dress, was dismounting at Paddington Station, his horse threw its head up and landed him on his back; it was cruel luck. I acted as Right Guide and was about ten yards behind the *kaiser* and all the kings and foreign representatives. I don't think any two of the household walked in step the whole way. I was clever enough to sneak into the service in the abbey, but they caught me on the steps of the chapel at Windsor and said that marshalling officers were no longer required!

In 1911 I went to Aldershot as Brigade-Major to the 6th (now 2nd) Brigade, commanded by Brigadier-General R. H. Davies, a New Zealander lent on exchange, a very practical man, whose goodness to me I can never forget.

The 6th Brigade consisted of the 60th Rifles (under Colonel Oxley and later Northey), the Leicestershire Regiment (under Lieutenant-Colonel Croker), the Hampshire Regiment (under Lieutenant-Colonel Jackson), the Royal Inniskilling Fusiliers (under Lieutenant-Colonel Hancox), later the South Staffordshire Regiment (under Lieutenant-Colonel Davidson) and my own regiment—The King's—(under Lieutenant-Colonel Bannatyne). We were always a very happy brigade. My brigadier, as I said above, was a very practical man from New Zealand, and he hated an office and every form of red tape. Whilst other brigade-majors were tied to their offices, I sometimes did not visit mine for days.

I used to take out papers, including courts martial, in my holsters, and we did our work in, the open during field days. He always made a practice of seeing the C.O.s daily and giving decisions on their various letters, which it was my business to confirm later in writing if necessary. It was that training which in later years of the Great War enabled me to do the same. I spent all my time, whether as G.S.O.1 of a division, B.G.G.S. of the Canadian Corps, or M.G.G.S. of the Second Army, out and about, always visiting headquarters and trenches, hearing commanders' difficulties and wants personally and, on return, confirming decisions in writing if necessary.

Sir Horace Smith-Dorrien was C.-in-C. at Aldershot at that time. On my first field day he rode up to me and said: "Is your name Harington?" On my replying that it was, he said: "I welcome you here and hope you will be very happy." I have never forgotten that, and during the last twenty years, when I have held many commands, I have always tried to do the same. In 1930, when I came home from India to be C.-in-C. at Aldershot, I was asked to take his son as *A.D.C.* I gladly did so. I did not know his son, but I took him on account of that kind act of his father when I was a very junior officer.

After Sir Horace Smith-Dorrien came Sir Douglas Haig, who was then and always, right through the war, very good to me.

As brigade-major, I remember so well the setting of schemes for majors to be tested in what was called "Tactical Fitness for Command". It was certainly an ordeal for them; they had to command a mixed force of cavalry, artillery and infantry, and they were given a scheme over country which, in most cases, they had never seen before. They were given a certain time in which to go away and consider what they would do. How often I used to tell a candidate that he need do just nothing; that he had got Jakes Harman and his squadron of Queen's Bays on his side and that was a certain winner, for Jakes Harman would gallop and capture Eelmoor Bridge long before anyone else, and the rest would be easy!

We certainly had some wonderful candidates. I remember one, from one of our dominions, arriving at the rendezvous at Fleet in a taxi-cab carrying a sword—no horse and no idea what it was all about! He could not read a map and would call everything by the wrong name, including Long Valley which he called "Short Valley". He only had to get thirty *per cent* marks but I am afraid that was too many. Another candidate was an officer from the War Office, a very clever man, but he had not been near troops for years. He ended by having his whole force, including his guns, surrounded and captured below Caesar's Camp; it was the most complete debacle, and he was ploughed. That was in 1913. By the end of 1914 he had won a glorious V.C. leading his battalion, at the head of which he was subsequently killed. So much for exams.

My time as brigade-major finished in December, 1913, and I rejoined my regiment in Talavera Barracks in the 6th Brigade. I put my company through field training and musketry in the spring of 1914, little thinking what was just ahead of us.

Sir Douglas Haig was so amused at my being back with my regiment doing company training that he used to ride round most mornings with his staff and friends to see what I was doing.

Another company in my regiment was commanded by my greatest friend, Captain Sheppard. We had great battles; once I stalked him all night round Fleet and other places; eventually I ran him to ground and captured him and his company while they were having breakfast just behind Government House.

In June, 1914, I was sent up to the War Office to help in revising the Field Service Regulations and, when the situation at the end of July became serious, I was transferred to the Mobilisation Branch, to help a tired and overworked staff under Brigadier-General Woodward. It was an education to me. I found two officers—Frith, R.E., and Wells, Loyal Regiment—who had, under Brigadier-General Woodward, worked out all the arrangements for mobilisation. The orders for "Precautionary Period" were issued shortly after my arrival, and then we waited.

On August 4th, after the fateful Cabinet Meeting, an undersecretary rushed in, saying: "Send out 'Mobilise'." How well do I remember Brigadier-General Woodward, without turning a hair, saying: "Go away and send me that in writing." It came back in writing. The Mobilisation Branch had had a faithful head clerk named Garrood, who for seventeen years had been working for this moment. I am proud to have followed that head clerk through the passages of the War Office, with Frith and Wells, and to have seen him hand in to C.I. the basket bearing the order "Mobilise"—the dream of his life. I was on duty that night—in fact I did not leave the War Office day or night for ten days—and let me say this: so perfect were the arrangements made by that branch under Frith and Wells that there was only one telephone call throughout the whole of that night, August 4-5, and that was a query about Richmond—was it Surrey or Yorkshire?

When released from that, I returned to the Victoria Hotel, Aldershot, where my wife was, and I mobilised and handed over my company in the regiment, and early one morning I saw my regiment march off from Talavera Barracks to entrain at Farnborough—so many dear friends never to return. It was commanded by Lieutenant-Colonel W. S. Bannatyne, who was killed early in the war—a great loss. He was a very fine soldier and a first-rate commanding officer and staff officer who would have gone far had he been spared.

The adjutant was Captain P. S. Hudson and the quartermaster was Captain Ball, who now runs the feeding at Wellington College so successfully.

In those days we had a lot of good cricketers in the regiment and, in July of that very year, the past and present of my regiment defeated a strong command side by seven wickets in a two-day match. Major E. G. Wynyard was playing for us. He was an instructor at Sandhurst when I was a cadet. Sheppard, Denham, Potter and I all joined The King's as cricketers, thanks to Teddy Wynyard. We all had very happy lives in the regiment, but it is sad to recall that seven of that side which beat the command in July, 1914, lost their lives in the war.

Those three years, 1911-14, as brigade-major and company commander at Aldershot, were full of interest. Training was at its highest. It was real hard work often night and day. Very good practical schemes were carried out, and I doubt if there was ever a better trained or better disciplined force than the army of that day. We little thought then how soon it was to be tested. Nothing except a very highly trained and disciplined force could have fought on as that force did at Mons and Le Cateau, or could have carried out that retreat in the way those men carried it out.

We must remember that the soldier of that day had only his rifle to rely on, and a very few machine-guns in each battalion; in addition, the soldier had to carry his kit.

Whilst giving full credit to the soldier of today we must not forget the soldier of 1914, who by his pluck and accurate rifle-shooting held back the Germans at the First Battle of Ypres. As one looks back now on the present war one remembers how glad we were in the early days that our B.E.F. had been safely landed and established alongside our French Allies and ready to be used should the Germans overrun the Belgians as in 1914. We little thought that the action or want of action by our French and Belgian Allies was soon to involve the B.E.F. in that terrible and historic Retreat on Dunkirk and the Coast to which I shall refer later. At any rate the pluck and spirit of the British soldier of 1914 was clearly shown again in 1940.

Shortly after mobilisation I was appointed G.S.O.2. to the El Corps, which was being formed under Lieutenant-General Pulteney (now Sir William Pulteney). It was to consist of the 4th and 6th Divisions, under Major-General D'Oyly Snow and Major-General Keir respectively. The B.G.G.S. was Brigadier-General Du Cane (as he then was). The G.S.O.1 was Colonel Maude (afterwards Sir Stanley Maude), G.S. 0.2 (I) Major (now Sir John) Davidson, G.S.O.3 Captain (now Lieutenant-General Sir William) Pitt-Taylor. The corps was formed during the Retreat from Mons, and consisted at that time of only die 4th Division and the 19th Brigade.

My first recollection of the III Corps was seeing with Brigadier-General Du Cane, some of the runaway horses from the Battle of Nery dashing themselves madly against a wall and killing themselves.

That retreat was something one can never forget. Day after day those poor, tired soldiers toiled on. We were going the wrong way. I remember one incident so well. Our C.R.A., Brigadier-General Phipps Hornby, V.C., and I were sent on, he to reconnoitre a gun position, I to select a headquarters. We rode on a long way and then he left me. I found what I thought would be a suitable headquarters at a farm, and there I waited for Head-quarters to arrive. I had a most uncanny and lonely feeling—just my groom and myself. At long last the corps commander and staff arrived, and they had hardly got out of their cars when we saw a party of *Uhlans* within a few hundred yards.

I shall never forget the *A.D.C.s*, the present Lords Lon-donderry and Pembroke, and myself and the chauffeurs, who had rifles but had probably never fired them before, all lying in the cabbages firing at the *Uhlans*. We each claimed to have hit one, but I am sure we never did. We learned afterwards that a German cavalry division or corps had just passed by within a mile. No wonder I had felt lonely. Luckily, I had not known.

We camped that night at Baron. We continued our retreat daily, and I remember an incident at Dammartin. We arrived there one night only to find that it had been General Sir John French's H.Q., and that he and his staff had just had to leave, ow-ing to the presence of the German cavalry. As far as I remember we had to move on also, but not till after we had eaten the din-ner which had been prepared for Sir John and his staff!

Then we got inside the defences of Paris, and I was sent on with some R.E. to arrange for the blowing up of all the bridges behind us. I came across a narrow culvert, wide enough to ride over, but not wide enough for a vehicle. I made all arrangements to blow it up, but when I reported it to the C.R.E., Brigadier-General Glubb, enquiries were made from Paris Headquarters, only to reveal that what I was proposing to blow up was the main water supply of Paris!

At long last when we were camped within the defences of Paris, the D.C.G.S., General Sir Archibald Murray, arrived one evening to say that the retreat was over, and that we would start to advance on the morrow to the Aisne. What joy! One could not believe they were the same soldiers that one saw the next day. The old spirit had returned. We were at last going the right way. And so, we advanced to Soissons on the Aisne.

We were held up there for some little time, and then it was decided to move the British Army to the north, to St. Omer and

Hazebrouck. I was sent up north to arrange for the arrival of the III Corps. I went in the Rolls Royce of Emmy Rothschild (extra *A.D.C.*). It was a good long journey, and all went well till I arrived at a little railway crossing short of St. Omer, where I was told that the Germans were in or around the town. I found the inhabitants in a state bordering on panic. The Germans were only a few miles off.

I stayed that night in a convent or hospital, I forget which, but I had the engine running all night in case of trouble. I sat up with the old French Territorial *commandant* most of the night, and he kept on saying: "Will the English be here in the morning?" I hoped just as much as he did that they would be. Much to my relief, the trains bringing the III Corps started to arrive next morning. The headquarters which I selected for the corps at St. Omer subsequently became Sir John French's Headquarters.

The corps then advanced to Hazebrouck. This advance was not without interest as the Germans were still in the neighbourhood of Strazeele, only a few miles away. They retired, and we marched on to Bailleul, where we established our headquarters in the town hall. We had, by then, been joined by the 6th Division, and the 4th and 6th Divisions advanced astride the Bailleul-Lille road towards Lille. So confident were we that we should go right forward to Lille that we moved our H.Q. into Armentières, but we were forced to return to Bailleul next day. Our advance had met with serious opposition, in which the Sherwood Foresters had very serious fighting at Ennetières.

I recollect so well Brigadier-General (the late General Sir Aylmer) Hunter Weston, who was then commanding the 11th Brigade, coming to beg the corps commander to return to Bailleul, as we were only a nuisance in Armentières. He was right.

We spent that winter with our H.Q. at Bailleul. The 4th Division H.Q. were at Nieppe, and the 6th at Bac St. Maur. It was during that winter that Lord Roberts paid us a visit, and I remember being told to explain to him the situation on a map in my office. He was suffering from a bad cold then, and he returned to G.H.Q. at St. Omer and died two or three days later.

About that time Brigadier-General (now General Sir John) Du Cane left us for G.H.Q., and he was succeeded by Brigadier-General (now Lord) Milne, and early in 1915 Colonel Maude (afterwards Sir Stanley) got command of an infantry brigade at Neuve Eglise. I had been G.S.O.2 to Colonel Maude since the start and had the greatest admiration for him; his subsequent death in Mesopotamia was a tragic loss to the army.

There was only one man who was glad when Joe Maude left us and that was our head clerk. He had been in the War Office, before the war, as confidential clerk to Sir William Robertson. He was used to putting on his hat in the War Office at 5 p.m. and going home, and he did not understand war. Colonel Maude was a man so full of energy that when he dictated an order, he expected it to be typed and issued in a moment. This was always too much for the head clerk, and when I told him that Colonel Maude had got a brigade and was leaving at once, this worthy clerk disappeared for two days. Whether, being Scotch, he expressed his joy in a beverage from that country I shall never know.

Brigadier-General Milne was succeeded by Brigadier-General Lynden Bell and, in April, I was sent as G.S.O.1 to the 49th West Riding Division on its arrival from England. I was succeeded by Lieutenant-Colonel (now General) W. H. Bartholomew. The 49th Division was commanded by MajorGeneral T. S. Baldock and was around Fleurbaix and Bac St. Maur.

We were first of all put into the line near Fleurbaix, in Lord Rawlinson's IV Corps and were on the left of the 8th Division in an attack made by that division which unfortunately did not succeed.

We were shortly afterwards moved up to the extreme left of the British line in the Ypres Salient in relief of the 4th Division, which had been engaged in very heavy fighting. It was a horrible part of the line, and we had a bad time building parapets and burying dead from the recent fighting. Our headquarters were at Trois Tours, near Brieleu. Our brigades were commanded by Brigadier-Generals Dawson, Macfarlane and Brereton. We had not been there long before we had a serious blow. I was returning from the trenches one afternoon when I saw an ambulance coming out of our H.Q. at Trois Tours, and found that it contained our divisional commander, Major-General Baldock, who had been seriously wounded in the head by shell-fire just outside headquarters. We were forced to move our headquarters to Hospital Farm, near Elverdinghe, and Major-General E. M. Perceval, then D.C.G.S., was appointed to command the division.

It was at this time that I made my first acquaintance with General (afterwards Lord) Plumer. Little did I think then of what was to happen later. Major-General Perceval got influenza and had to be taken into hospital in Hazebrouck and a heavy responsibility fell on me. I was, I think, the only regular officer in the division at the time and General Plumer used to visit us almost every day. One day he told me that I was to command a brigade in the 14th Division at Hooge, in place of Brigadier-General Oliver Nugent who was getting the Ulster Division.

I was just going to England for five days' leave, from which I came back prepared and equipped to spend a bad time at Hooge, but I was met at Boulogne by a staff officer with a megaphone, who told me to report, and then informed me that my brigade had been cancelled by Sir William Robertson (then C.G.S.) and that I was to go to Bailleul as B.G.G.S. of the Canadian Corps which was being formed. I reported *en route* to the military secretary at G.H.Q., who told me that I had been previously selected for B.G.G.S. 12th Corps, going to Salonika, but that owing to Major-General Perceval being in hospital I could not be spared, and so Major-General Bols was sent to the 12th Corps, as the matter was urgent, and I was retained for the Canadian Corps. In fact, General Percival's influenza altered my whole career!

I shall never forget my arrival at the Canadian Corps at Bailleul. The corps, which had only been formed that day, was commanded by Lieutenant-General Alderson of Mounted Infantry fame. I had never met him before. Seely (now Lord Mottistone) commanded the Canadian Cavalry Brigade. The corps at the moment was only the 1st Canadian Division, just handed over from Alderson to Currie, and the Cavalry Brigade. Brigadier-General Wood was A.A. and Q.M.G. There was no general staff, or rather none had arrived, and the head clerk had lost his uniform and appeared in plain clothes and a bowler hat!

The corps was in the line near Messines. Major Ross Hayter arrived next day as G.S.O.2 and Major Mitchell as Intelligence Officer. The 2nd Canadian Division arrived shortly afterwards under Major-General Turner, V.C., and later the 3rd Division under Major-General Lipsett, and later still the 4th Division under Major-General Mercer.

I think I am right in saying that the first real raid was made by the 7th Canadian Battalion under Lieutenant-Colonel Odium and was a complete success. I visited the raiding party shortly before the raid, and promised them a week's leave if they succeeded, which they did. The army refused the leave, but they got it in the end. Early in 1916 the Canadian Corps was ordered to move up to the Ypres Salient in relief of the V Corps.

I think it was the first time that a whole corps had relieved another corps. It involved an enormous amount of staff work, but we got through successfully and eventually moved our H.Q. to Abeele. We had some very heavy fighting about Hill 60 and the St. Eloi craters.

I lost a good friend over that relief. For days before we moved up, Major Beatty (a brother of Lord Beatty), who was an *A.D.C.* to Lieutenant-General Alderson, and I used to go up and reconnoitre parts of our new corps line. Two nights before we took over, there had been heavy fighting on the right of the 5th Corps near St. Eloi, and our machine-guns had co-operated from our extreme left. Beatty came in to see if I was coming, but I was too busy with orders for the move, and, as he wanted a task, I asked him to go up to our extreme left and find out what our machine-guns had done. Whilst there he was buried by a shell and lost his arm. A few weeks later it took a turn for the worse and he died.

In the spring of 1916, Lieutenant-General Alderson left and was succeeded by Lieutenant-General Sir Julian (afterwards

Lord) Byng from the cavalry corps. I shall always remember his arrival. He was so keen to get round the front line at once, and the very night he took over we spent a most unpleasant time in the St. Eloi sector with enemy machine-guns extra busy. Next morning, we started on a tour of all divisional and brigade head-quarters, and at the 4th Division he gave General Mercer orders to make a reconnaissance in the neighbourhood of Mt. Sorrel, with a view to straightening out our line, into which the enemy had forced a wedge.

In the afternoon we were having tea in Brigadier-General Williams' H.Q. in railway dugouts when Major-General Mercer, his divisional commander, came in to discuss that reconnaissance with him. I remember the conversation so well. Major-General Mercer turned to the corps commander and said: "Williams and I are going up tomorrow, general, to make that reconnaissance; will you come?" Knowing General Byng's anxiety to see eve-rything to do with the front line at once, I naturally expected to hear him say "Yes". Instead, he paused for quite a long time, which surprised me greatly, and then he said: "No, you and Wil-liams go tomorrow and make your plans, and Tim and I will come up on Saturday." It was then Thursday afternoon. It was a right decision, he had only just met them that day and he did not want to be in their way, or cramp their style.

It had a tragic sequel. It is easy to be wise afterwards, but I can still remember that the shelling that afternoon, when we visited various. Brigade H.Q. in front of Ypres, was much heavier than usual. It was really a preliminary bombardment. Mercer and Wil-liams were up in the line about 3 a.m. next morning, 3rd June, 1916, when the attack on Mt. Sorrel developed. Mercer and some of his staff were killed; Williams was seriously wounded and taken prisoner; the Germans captured Mt. Sorrel. If General Byng had said "Yes", as I expected, instead of "No", I should not be writing this story. Mt. Sorrel was a very important and com-manding position in front of Ypres. It dominated our defences, and in German hands it was a serious menace to the defence of the Ypres Salient. It was essential to recover it.

A few days afterwards, at Abeele, General Byng told me that I had been selected as M.G.G.S. Second Army to General Plumer. I had never even given a thought to such a thing, but when General Plumer visited the Canadian Corps H.Q. next day I naturally thanked him for his kindness in selecting me; whereupon he replied, as quick as lightning: "I won't have you at all unless you get Mt. Sorrel back!" We got it back.

At the time. Sir Douglas Haig, as he then was, was preparing for an advance down south and could ill afford to send any reinforcements to us in the north. One 6-in. howitzer brigade was, indeed, all we got. Very careful preparations, however, were made for the hill to be retaken by the Canadians themselves, aided by this howitzer brigade, and the main task was entrusted to Major-General Lipsett.

Early on the morning of 13th June, 1916, the attack was launched and was a complete success. In my opinion it was the most brilliant bit of work done by the Canadians in the whole war. Serious losses were inflicted on the enemy, and Mt. Sorrel was recaptured. That day I handed over my job as B.G.G.S. to Brigadier-General P. de B. Radcliffe and went straight off to Cassel to take over M.G.G.S. to General Plumer.

What a happy and wonderful experience I had with the Canadian Corps. Such grand fellows! I made friendships during that time which can never be broken. I have kept them up ever since. My dear friend Currie, who died a few years back, Burstall (C.R.A.), Armstrong (C.R.E.), Mitchell (Intelligence), afterwards with me in the Second Army, and so many others. I found it difficult at first as politics seemed to play such a part. Sir Sam Hughes sent instructions from Canada as regards the command of brigades, etc. Max Aitken (now Lord Beaverbrook) was "Eye Witness" and played a big part, especially as regards the "Ross Rifle".

Whilst I have the greatest admiration for the Ross Rifle as a rifle on a range, it could not stand the mud, slime, and slush of the Ypres Salient. Before the Canadian Corps was formed, the 1st Canadian Division had got permission to exchange it for our

Lee-Enfield.

I remember a conference on the merits of each, when Brigadier-General Currie was asked his opinion and said: "It (the Ross Rifle) may be a good rifle, but the b——y thing won't shoot." The 2nd, 3rd, and 4th Canadian Divisions were not allowed to exchange it for the Lee-Enfield, and I have seen men crying with rage at being sent into the trenches in the Ypres Salient with a rifle which they knew would jam, and I know how they tried to borrow or buy rifles from the neighbouring British troops. In the end, the army commander ordered a secret vote to be taken, from platoon commanders upwards, as to their views on the subject of the Ross versus the Lee-Enfield. I had to collect the votes and burn all records. The voting was some ninety-six *per cen*t in favour of the Lee-Enfield, and the exchange was. The odd four *per cent* were politicians and thought only of their future. I am afraid that many lives were lost before that transfer.

It is a curious thing that when I came home from Gibraltar a man on board the P. & O. came up and said: "You won't remember me!" When he gave me his name, I said: "Don't I! You were the C.O. who refused to take your battalion into the trenches unless you got the Lee-Enfield Rifle." At Bisley, only recently, at the meeting of the N.R.A., of which I am a vice-president, I dined with the Canadian Rifle team and my next-door neighbour told me how, in the Great War, he used to take two rifles up to the trenches—the Ross and the Lee-Enfield—but he would not tell me from what source he got the latter!

I have already referred to the arrival of General Byng and his anxiety to get to know everything and everybody. He was a great personality and inspired everyone. In those days the Canadian Corps was not famed for saluting. We issued orders on the subject without any effect, until one day at the Corps School, General Byng remarked quietly in his droll way that he thought things were improving and that he had noticed that most of the men whom he saluted, answered him back! We had no further bother as regards saluting!

He was a very wonderful man, as Canada herself was to learn

later, when he became governor-general. His goodness to me I can never forget. At Abeele once, at the time of the Mt. Sorrel fighting, knowing that I was bothered all night by telephone calls, and wanting me to get a good night's rest, he, as corps commander, insisted upon going on night duty. He had his camp bed moved into the office and the telephone put alongside, and he sent me to bed in my hut.

Next morning, when I went in, he said: "Tim, I haven't had a single call all night," and seemed much surprised. Of course, he hadn't. Was it likely that I was going to have the corps commander rung up all night! I had the telephone and his was a dud, but what a grand man to try and do such a thing! Just characteristic of the man. The Canadians loved him, and rightly so.

That reminds me of another story about him. H.R.H. the Duke of Connaught was to have presented prizes at my old school, Cheltenham College, soon after the war, but he was indisposed and could not go. I was deputed to get a distinguished soldier, so I got Lord Byng. He started his speech by saying that he could not think why he had been asked, as he had been at Eton, and had been bottom of Eton until his great friend Harry Rawlinson (Lord Rawlinson) had taken his place! What he principally remembered about Eton was swopping a pair of trousers and a pineapple for two guinea pigs! The boys simply loved him and followed him about all over the playground trying to get his autograph.

The whole nation has been stirred to the core at the warmth of the welcome given to our king and queen during their visit to Canada and the United States, but those of us who, like myself, had the privilege of serving with the gallant Canadians in the Great War can perhaps picture that welcome more clearly. It must have been quite wonderful, for they are a wonderful people and never forget one. I have kept in touch with many since those days, and I hope very much that I shall be able to visit that great country at a later date. They have asked me twice, and only recently they wired to ask me if I could go to Toronto on Empire Day to take the salute of 40,000 ex-Canadian Corps soldiers. I only wish it had been possible. My regiment (The King's) is allied to the Toronto Grenadiers, and I shall always remember that this regiment sent a detachment of officers and men, at its own expense, to take part with my regiment in the Aldershot Tattoo when I was C.-in-C. at Aldershot.

The response to the nation's call for this war has shown "Canada at her best". She has sent us truly magnificent contingents. I have been privileged to meet many. I have also the honour of being president of the Canadian Ex-Servicemen's Association in England. Not only has Canada sent over these fine troops but the great task of training pilots from our Dominions is being carried out in Canada today. It was reported recently that the Germans had deliberately damaged the Canadian war memorial on Vimy Ridge. It is more than likely that the Germans will have cause to regret that monstrous act before very long.

THE SECOND ARMY

On 13th June, 1916, I went to the Second Army. Little did I think what a wonderful association I was starting that day, or what the next two years were to mean to me with the marvellous opportunity of living in such close touch with such a leader and commander, and of studying the way in which he gained the affection of all ranks in the old Second Army.

I remember being terribly frightened at the task before me. I had never thought in "Armies". When I was a student at the Staff College, only ten years before, we never, even in theory, dealt with, or thought of a force exceeding our Expeditionary Force of six divisions. A corps of four divisions had seemed enormous, but here I was confronted with the Staff work of an army which, two or three times in my tenure, exceeded thirty divisions!

As Chief General Staff Officer of the 49th Division and Canadian Corps I had been able to keep in touch with the front line and subordinate commanders, but I visualisd an Army Headquarters as quite another picture. I thought it would be much more like the War Office, where one sat and issued all sorts of orders and instructions which, if they ever reached the regimental officer in the front line, would be ridiculed. I found something quite different.

I found that the army commander himself travelled a hundred miles a day round the army, visiting corps, divisional, brigade, and often battalion H.Q., seeing units coming out of the line, visiting units in rest; and I was soon doing the same the other way round the army. We used to meet at some appointed H.Q., and, by this method, very few units in the Second Army were ever omitted. The system, however, went much further. The army commander believed in having only one officer in each branch actually on duty at army headquarters; the rest had to be out visiting, and seeing what the troops actually wanted, and their situation.

The M.G.A., Major-General Chichester, the C.R.E., Major-General Glubb, the C.R.A., Major-General Franks, the Chief Signal Officer, Brigadier-General Hildebrand, the Chief Intelligence Officer, Brigadier-General Mitchell, and their Staffs were all travelling round every day with the password: "Out to help." We had another pass-word: "Never to spy."

It was the strict observance of the latter which made us welcome everywhere.

You may ask what was the good of all this visiting, so I will give you the answer. Every morning, and in the winter every evening, the army commander held a conference of all the heads of departments. It always opened with an account by the chief of the intelligence staff of the general situation of our own forces and of those of the enemy. Then, each in turn, we gave the results of our own tours, and what various commanders had told us and asked for, and our own suggestions. By this means the army commander kept in the closest touch, and on his daily tour went off to see for himself the various points of interest or discussion, taking with him the senior staff or departmental officer concerned.

I saw the review of a book, issued recently, by a staff officer, whom I don't think I ever met, on staff work in the war, in which he emphasises the fact that the commanders or staffs in formation above a division had little or no influence on the lower formations, or on the troops themselves. I think that if the author had served in the Second Army under General Plumer, he might have taken a different view. Having had thirty-three miles of front to hold, of which I was proud to know every yard, and having had junior army staff officers three or four nights a week in various sectors "out to help" in every way and keep the army commander in the closest touch, I am afraid that I cannot share the opinion of the author on that point, although I am told that the book is most helpful.

It is true that in his book *Realities of War* Sir Philip Gibbs makes some very severe criticism of many of our commanders and staff officers and the feeling against them in many of the lower formations. The members of the Second Army Staff were a family under the guidance and direction of their old chief, Lord Plumer.

It is in order to do justice to that Staff, who did the work and bore the brunt, and in no way to claim any credit for my own humble efforts, that I reproduce the following from Sir Philip Gibbs' book:

As there are exceptions to every rule, so harsh criticism must be modified in favour of the generalship and organisation of the Second Army—of rare efficiency under the restrictions and authority of the general staff. I often used to wonder what qualities belonged to Sir Herbert Plumer, the army commander. In appearance he was almost a caricature of an old-time British general, with his ruddy, pippin-cheeked face, with white hair and a fierce little white moustache, and blue, watery eyes, and a little pot-belly and short legs. He puffed and panted when he walked, and after two minutes in his company Cyril Maude would have played him to perfection. The staff work of his army was as good in detail as any machinery of war may be, and the tactical direction of the Second Army battles was not slip-shod or haphazard, as so many others, but prepared with minute attention to detail and after thoughtful planning of the general scheme.

The Battle of Wyteschaete and Messines was a model in organisation and method, and worked in its frightful destructiveness like the clockwork of a death machine. Even the battles of Flanders in the autumn of 1917, ghastly as they were in the losses of our men, in the state of the ground through which they had to fight, and in the futile results, were well organized by the Second Army Headquarters, compared with the abominable mismanagement of other troops, the contrast being visible to every battalion officer and even to the private soldier. How much share of this was due to Sir Herbert Plumer it is impossible for me to tell, though it is fair to give him credit for soundness of judgment in general ideas, and in the choice of men.

He had for his Chief of Staff Sir Charles Harington, and beyond all doubt this general was the organising brain of the Second Army, though with punctilious chivalry he gave, always, the credit of all his work to the army commander. A thin, nervous, highly-strung man, with extreme simplicity of manner and clarity of intelligence, he impressed me as a brain of the highest temper and quality in Staff work. His memory for detail was like a card-index system, yet his mind was not clogged with detail, but saw the wood as well as the trees, and the whole broad sweep of the problem which confronted him. There was something fascinating as well as terrible in his exposition of a battle that he was planning. For the first time, in his presence and over his maps, I saw that, after all, there was such a thing as the science of war, and that it was not always a fetish of elementary ideas raised to the nth degree of pomposity, as I had been led to believe by contact with other generals and staff officers.

Here at least was a man who dealt with it as a scientific business, according to the methods of science—calculating the weight and effect of gunfire, the strength of the enemy's defences and man-power, the psychology of German generalship and of German units, the pressure which could be put on British troops before the breaking-point of courage, the relative, or cumulative effects of poison gas, mines, heavy and light artillery, tanks, the disposition of German guns, and the probability of their movement in this direction or that, the amount of their wastage under our counter-battery work, the advantages of attack in depth—one body of troops 'leap-frogging' another in an advance to further objectives—the time-table of transport, the supply of food and water and ammunition, the comfort of troops before action, and a thousand other factors of success.

Before every battle fought by the Second Army, and on the eve of it, Sir Charles Harington sent for the war correspondents and devoted an hour or more to a detailed explanation of his plans. He put down all his cards on the table, with perfect candour, hiding nothing, neither minimising nor exaggerating the difficulties and danger of the attack, pointing out the tactical obstacles which must be overcome before any chance of success, and exposing the general strategy in the simplest and clearest speech.

I used to study him at those times, and marvelled at him. After intense and prolonged work at all this detail involving the lives of thousands of men, he was highly wrought, with every nerve in his body and brain at full tension, but he was never flurried, never irritable, never depressed or elated by false pessimism or false optimism. He was a chemist explaining the factors of a great experiment of which the result was still uncertain. He could only hope for certain results after careful analysis and synthesis. Yet he was not dehumanised. He laughed sometimes at surprises he had caused the enemy or was likely to cause them— surprises which would lead to a massacre of their men. He warmed to the glory of the courage of the troops who were carrying out his plans. He would say:

> It depends on these fellows. We are setting them a
> difficult job. If they can do it, as I hope and believe,
> it will be a fine achievement. They have been very
> much tried, poor fellows, but their spirit is still high,
> as I know from their commanding officers.

One of his ambitions was to break down the prejudice
between the fighting units and the staff.

> We want them to know that we are all working
> together, for the same purpose, and with the same
> zeal. They cannot do without us, as we cannot do
> without them, and I want them to feel that the
> work done here is to help them to do theirs more
> easily, with lighter losses, in better physical condi-
> tions, with organisation behind them at every stage.

Many times, the Second Army would not order an attack
or decide the time of it before consulting the divisional
generals and brigadiers, and obtaining their consensus of
opinion. The officers and men in the Second Army did
actually come to acknowledge the value of the staff work
behind them, and felt a confidence in its devotion to their
interests which was rare on the Western Front.

At the end of one of his expositions Sir Charles Harington would rise and gather up his maps and papers and say:

> Well; there you are, gentlemen. You know as much
> as I do about the plans for tomorrow's battle. At the
> end of the day, you will be able to see the result of all
> our work, and tell me things I do not know.

I value very much an album which was given to me after the
Battle of Messines. It contains the following inscription:

> To Major-General C. H. Harington, C.B., D.S.O.,
> Chief of Staff, Second Army.

With compliments and grateful acknowledgements of
generous and invaluable assistance before and after the

glorious Battle of Messines from the War Correspondents with the British Armies in the Field.

It contains all the Press cuttings of the Battle of Messines and is signed in the following order by:

H. Perry Robinson (*The Times, Daily News*, etc.).

W. Beach Thomas (*The Daily Mail*, etc.).

Percival Phillips (*The Morning Post, Daily Express*, etc.).

Philip Gibbs (*The Daily Chronicle, Daily Telegraph*, etc.).

Herbert Russell (Reuters and Press Association).

Wm. Philip Simmons (United Press of America).

De Witt Mackenzie (The Associated Press of America).

It was my privilege as M.G.G.S. to attend with the army commander the conferences held by Sir Douglas Haig with all the army commanders. Each army commander in turn described the situation on his own front, and Sir Douglas Haig on the general situation. Though handicapped by being a bad speaker, his summary of the situation was always excellent. He was an intense student of war.

I remember a conference on 7th May, 1917, when he told us that the Second Army was to capture the Messines Ridge, for which we had been making preparations for some time beforehand, and he asked General Plumer the earliest date he could do it. Plumer replied: "Today month, sir." We returned to Cassel in great heart, and we did indeed spend a busy month.

There was not a detail of those preparations which the army commander himself did not supervise. Every gun position, every light railway for ammunition, every railhead, hospital and back arrangements he visited. He consulted corps, divisional, and brigade commanders as to the best hour to attack, the pace of the barrage, and the various objectives and other details, and then decided himself and told me to issue the orders. It was a wonderful example, as, before the attack, every subordinate commander was able to feel that he had at any rate been consulted and that no doubt the final decision was the best.

The artillery arrangements under our C.R.A., Major-General Franks, were wonderful. We had the greatest concentration of guns at that time known in history—one gun to seven yards, if I remember rightly. We also had some twenty to thirty mines which had, for a year or more, been bored under the whole Messines Ridge. I had frequently walked under the Ridge.

During all my time with the army commander, who went to bed punctually at 9.30 p.m., I only called him twice in the night. The first time was in February, 1917, when our O.C. Mines, Colonel (late Major-General) Stevenson, came down to me and said that we must blow our mines under Hill 60 at once as the Germans were within a few feet. I knocked on the army commander's door and told him: "'Mines' says we must blow the Hill 60 mines tonight."

The army commander replied: "I won't have them blown. Goodnight."

They were not blown; they lived to be blown at 2.50 a.m. on 7th June, in the attack on Messines. It was a fine and brave decision.

I always remember the eve of the Battle of Messines—bed at 9.30 p.m.—breakfast at 2.30 a.m. I can see now the glare in the sky as the mines went up. The army commander was not with us; he was on his knees in his room, praying for those gallant men who were scaling the Ridge. Presently reports began to come in—all favourable. The troops had been successful all along the line. The Messines-Wytschaete Ridge, under which our troops had lived since the winter of 1914, was ours at last. Looking down the ridge, which I visited next morning, it was impossible to imagine that our troops could have lived all that time, commanded at every turn by that high ground. The explosion must have been terrific. The crater at Spanbrokemolen, which had been preserved, was an amazing sight.

In a German concrete dugout, close by, I saw four German officers sitting up round a table—all dead—killed by shock. In an officer's pocket was found the copy of a message he had actually sent at 2.50 a.m. saying: "Situation comparatively quiet." He literally was living on a volcano, poor fellow. The pleasing feature of that day was that all objectives were taken, and that our losses were only about one-tenth of what we had expected and feared. Congratulations poured in to the army commander from all sides. Messages from King George and the Duke of Connaught, on whose staff the army commander had served, were much appreciated.

Much has been written about that battle, and critics have been generally very kind. It was, however, only an operation with a "limited objective". It was designed to accomplish a certain task, namely to place the ridge firmly in our hands, and it succeeded. To my mind the main lesson to be learned from Messines is "Thoroughness in Preparation". As I said previously, the army commander kept his finger on the pulse of everything, and all of us who were privileged to serve under him had to see that no detail, however small, was omitted. He told me once that any success he ever had was due to having been Q.M.G. of the army. He understood the value of the "Back Arrangements", as I call them, and he saw to them all himself. That is why troops liked coming into his Second Army; it gave them confidence.

There were many examples in the Great War of operations, from trench raids up to battles on the largest scale, failing for want of thorough preparation. Attacks went well up to a point and success seemed assured, and then something went wrong behind—feeding, perhaps, or transport, or reserves not available at the right time or place—just something which nullified the initial success—so that the whole operation crumbled. I think that is the lesson of the war—the majority of operations well prepared succeeded—the majority of operations ill-prepared failed.

The capture of the Messines-Wytschaete Ridge made it possible for Sir Douglas Haig to push on with his major project of advancing through Belgium to the coast. As I write I can see that commanding position of Passchendaele standing in the way. Of that more later. I think my chief rather hoped that, after Messines, he might have been entrusted with the task of the further advance, but it was not given to him. It was given, at first, to Lord Rawlinson who, with his M.G.G.S., General Archie Montgomery, as he then was, came up to reconnoitre with that object. Later, however, changes were made and the task was entrusted to the Fifth Army under Sir Hubert Gough, to whom we were ordered to hand over several corps, including the corps holding Ypres, which had always been under the command of the Second Army. The Second Army was reduced to four corps only, holding the front south of St. Eloi, what may be called the Broodseinde Front.

The operations for the capture of Passchendaele then began and, on October 4th, a combined attack by the Second and Fifth Armies was made. The Second Army captured all its objectives, including the Broodseinde Ridge, and I have always said that that operation was the best ever carried out by the Second Army. We had very little time to prepare, compared with the operation of Messines.

The Fifth Army, on our left, met with serious opposition and made little progress. Unfortunately, at this time the weather broke and got worse and worse. Sir Douglas Haig, usually accompanied by his chief of staff, used to come up to Cassel almost daily and hold conferences with the commanders of the Second and Fifth Armies in my office as I had the best map. Sir Douglas was determined to get Passchendaele before winter if it was possible.

Various changes were made, and several corps of the Fifth Army were handed over to the Second Army, which was now entrusted with the major role. Several attempts were made. The weather was just appalling. We encountered serious opposition at Bellevue, on the way up to Passchendaele, the 49th West Riding Division and the New Zealanders suffering very heavily. General Gough was, I know, opposed to the attempts in such weather; he rang me up at about two-thirty one night, on the eve of an attack, and wanted me to ask General Plumer to stop it. The latter came down to my room and waited while I rang up and asked the opinion of each of our corps commanders.

They all, with one exception, who did not express a definite opinion, agreed that it was then impossible to stop the attack as the infantry had already been on the move for hours, and it would be impossible to get orders to them. General Plumer then took the telephone and I remember his words so well: "Is that you, Gough? The attack must go on. I am responsible, not you. Goodnight and good luck." Another big decision. We eventually got Passchendaele on 9th November, 1917. No one deplores all that fighting more than I do; I was the unfortunate Staff Officer who had to issue the orders for the greater part of it.

That advance to Passchendaele gave the critics the chance to belittle and damage the reputation of the great men who bore that awful responsibility. It may be that no advance should ever have been made after Messines in June, and that nothing more should have been attempted till the following year. I do not know, as I know nothing about the higher strategy, or the arrangements made with, or the conditions of, our Allies. It may be that it was considered to be essential to get Passchendaele Ridge as a jumping-off place for the following spring offensive to the coast. I do not know, but I contend that after the capture of Broodseinde and the subsequent advance and hold up at Bellevue, close under Passchendaele, there was no place where the army could have stopped for the winter and been maintained.

I asked, in my *Life of Lord Plumer*, if anyone could suggest a line on which we could have stopped; I have never seen a reply. I had personally reconnoitred all that ground under the most appalling conditions and I feel sure that if he had been with me on the Gravenstafel Ridge, the most violent critic of Passchendaele would not have voted for staying there for the winter, or even for any more minutes than necessary.

As an instance of his thoroughness, I recall General Plumer's great interest in all our Second Army Schools. How well I remember our Musketry School near St. Omer, our Sniping School under Major Slater at Mt. des Cats, our Trench Mortar and other schools. I recall the ten-day courses for C.O.s and also for adjutants, which not only gave them a rest from the line but also gave them an insight into what went on behind an army. The army commander always addressed these courses himself.

I have always ascribed Lord Plumer's successful operations

to three "Ts"—Trust, Training and Thoroughness. They, in my opinion, always stood out. He spared no effort to inspire and gain the trust of everyone under him. He realised the value of that trust, and no one can deny that he gained it. This was particularly emphasised by the way in which the troops of our great Dominions loved and trusted him. He had won their admiration in the South African War and they had not forgotten him. As regards training, he knew its value. He would have nothing left to chance; everyone must know his job, and I have stressed above, his thoroughness and knowledge of every detail; there was no trusting to luck with him. Above all was his own great trust in God.

ITALY

Soon after the capture of Passchendaele the army commander sent for me and, on my entering, exclaimed: "You and I have got the sack. Rawly takes over the Second Army tomorrow." He loved to get a rise out of me, and he certainly did that time! Then he showed me a telegram ordering us both to Italy. It was just after Caporetto. Lord Cavan and a corps staff had already gone in advance of any troops, but presumably it had been decided to send an army commander, and my chief had been selected. Mr. Lloyd George was in Paris, at the Hotel Meurice, and we were summoned to see him *en route*. We learnt that five British divisions had been ordered from the Western Front to Italy and that Mr. Lloyd George favoured reinforcing that front.

There was an amusing incident on our journey to Padua. We had arranged to dine quietly in the refreshment-room at Milan, but to our horror, as the train pulled up there, we found the station beflagged and thousands of people on the platform. The military secretary was sure that it was a welcome to our chief, who was hastily making ready to cope with it, when the railway staff officer informed us that it had nothing whatever to do with us; it was a "send off" to the first wounded Italian soldiers returning to the Front! We made our way through the crowd and had our dinner in peace.

On our arrival at Padua, we were met by Lord Cavan, Brigadier-General Gathorne-Hardy, B.G.G.S., and the Duke of Windsor, who was then Staff Captain XIV Corps. Padua was in rather a state of panic as they thought the Austrians were quite near; all the waiters had just fled from the hotel. Marshal Foch and Weygand were there, and Sir Henry Wilson; Sir William Robertson had just left. General Diaz was the new Italian C.-in-C., and one of his staff officers was Badoglio, the Victor of Abyssinia. He and I became great friends as I did a lot of work with him. He looked so young that I called him my G.S.O.3.

I often had tea with him when we were discussing matters, and he had his servants dressed in white. One day the man who was handing me tea saw me hesitate for a moment and he promptly said: "Sugar, sir;" I said: "Where did you learn English so well;" He replied: "I was a waiter, sir, for sixteen years at the Hyde Park Hotel before the war."

We had many conferences with General Diaz and gradually learnt the situation. Brigadier Delmé-Radcliffe was our *attaché*, or liaison officer, with the Italian Army. The French had their Headquarters also in Padua. A few days after we got there the British troops began to arrive, the first being the 23rd Division under Major-General Babington. We were not destined to remain long in Padua, as the Austrian bombers soon got news of all three headquarters being there and bombed us at intervals of half an hour.

The fact that my chief, Major-General Percival, had a cold and was in hospital at Hazebrouck, once altered the whole of my career, for it sent me to the Canadian Corps instead of to Salonika. Now at Padua I was saved by having a cold myself. Only, I think, twice when I was with General Plumer, did I not go back to my office after dinner, but one night at Padua I had such a heavy cold that General Plumer definitely ordered me to bed.

About 9.30 p.m. enemy bombers dropped a bomb through my office, killing the sentry outside, wounding a clerk, and wrecking my office. I should certainly have got that one. We were really very lucky that night, for another bomb fell between my office and the staff mess the other side of the road which was full of officers. We moved to a large house about six miles out, and the British troops soon afterwards took over the line at Montello.

Our house in Padua brings back memories. My old chief hated a telephone and would never speak through one if he could help it. When we first moved in, we hid the telephone in the chief's room, under his writing-table, where it went off later. I think Major Knowles, the A.M.S., got the blame for that!

It was the coldest house I have ever lived in. There were no fire-places but there was a wall, and I presume a chimney, against which one could burn logs; our trouble was to get the logs to blaze. One day our A.M.S., complete in staff uniform and staff hat, was seen in a shop in Padua on his knees blowing out his cheeks! Like the rest of us he knew no Italian, but he got the bellows he was out to buy for our comfort, and we owe him a great debt of gratitude.

I came home on a few days' leave at Christmas, and one day I was astonished to get a message asking me to breakfast with the prime minister. There were only Mr. Lloyd George, Lord Carson and Sir Maurice Hankey present. We had a charming breakfast, and Mr. Lloyd George, whom I had only met once before, in Paris, was most kind.

We came to the end of breakfast, and I was still wondering why I had been asked, when Mr. Lloyd George sat back and said: "Now, General, tell us how you would win the war!"

I was somewhat taken aback and explained that I had no idea of the situation on other fronts, but still hoped that the operations on the Western Front, which had been dormant since Passchendaele, would succeed in the spring. I had said exactly the wrong thing, and was very soon outside the door.

Mr. Lloyd George, who hated everything to do with the Western Front and favoured the smaller fronts, presumably wanted me to suggest sending more troops to Italy for a big offensive. As a matter of fact, General Plumer soon after sent back two divisions to the Western Front as he did not require them.

Before I returned to Italy, I was sent for to the War Office and told confidentially that a wire had been sent to General Plumer, offering him the post of C.I.G.S. in succession to Sir William Robertson, but that there was a snag in it as it only gave him some restricted powers, and not an entirely free hand. On this I wired to General Plumer asking him to await my arrival. He met me at Milan and I asked him if he had got the War Office wire; he said; "Oh yes, and I answered it at once." On enquiring what he had said, he replied: "Refused, of course." He had seen the snag all right.

Our stay in Italy soon terminated. We were delighted when, early in March, we received orders to hand over to Lord Cavan, who was to be raised to the status of an army commander, and to return to our old Second Army at Cassel, once more to be responsible for the Ypres Salient. I think we got back on March 13th, but as I have never kept a diary or a note, everything in this book, except for certain letters and documents, has to be written from memory.

It makes one sad as one looks back. There were the British troops hurrying to the aid of the Italians, our old and valued friends, and being welcomed by them. I was privileged with Lord Plumer to be received and honoured by the King of Italy. In later years I was privileged to have the Italian troops in Constantinople under my command, when I commanded the Allied Forces of Occupation. I am convinced that our respective nations would much rather be friends. We always have been. We fought alongside each other in the last war. We have no reason whatever to quarrel with Italy—nor had France—and yet we witnessed Mussolini, who had done great things for his country, being literally pulled along by the nose by Hitler and made to declare war on France and Great Britain.

That France or the Petain Government was prepared to eat dirt at the hands of Mussolini and surrender after twelve days without a fight is the concern of France alone, but Mussolini may well have cause to regret his "under the belt" action before very long. We hear a lot about the Italian mastery of the Mediterranean. That can hardly be gained by sitting in harbour and being too late to come out as at Oran. Mussolini's trouble is that there is a British Fleet in the Mediterranean which appears to get terribly in his way.

The same applied to Franco in the recent Spanish War which made our position in Gibraltar very difficult at times.

The Second Army, on our return, consisted of some fourteen strong divisions, including the Australian Corps, which was holding the Messines Ridge. Then came the 21st March—the worst day the British Army ever had in its history—and the German attack on the Third and Fifth Armies. I accompanied my chief that night to Montreuil to see Sir Douglas Haig. He told us the latest situation, and I can picture my old chief now, in front of a map on the wall with his hand on Sir Douglas's shoulder, offering all the help he could. He offered twelve divisions and I remember Sir Douglas saying: "That means giving up Passchendaele." "Not a bit of it," was his reply.

It was a very moving scene—the older man trying to help the younger one who was bearing that awful responsibility. We were not long in sending off those divisions, and in their place, we got the remnants of the very tired and weak divisions which had been through the fighting of the 21st. In a few days the Messines Ridge, instead of being held by four strong Australian divisions, was held by four weak and weary brigades.

It was too much in the end. The Germans, elated by their success in the south in their attempt to drive a wedge between the British and French, decided to try a minor operation in the north, presumably to prevent reinforcements from being sent south. It had been decided that our Second Army was to extend its right and take over the left division of the First Army, and I had accompanied my chief to a conference with the Commander of the IX Corps, General Haking. The Portuguese were on the left of the First Army and a division was actually *en route* by train from the south to replace them, is they were due for relief.

As luck would have it the attack was launched against the

Portuguese that night and then was extended against the right of the Second Army. Our tired troops could not stop the enemy advance, and had to give way. I felt so sorry for my old chief having to give up Passchendaele, Messines, Kemmel, Bailleul and all the places which had been ours so long. The enemy pressed right through to Meteren. Marshal Foch sent up some French reinforcements to help us.

I remember telling the army commander one night that our old army was in three pieces, as the enemy had broken through on each side of Meteren, and he replied: "Well, that's better than being in four." Such was his great spirit. About this time, I was appointed D.C.I.G.S. to Sir Henry Wilson, but I was allowed to remain in France until the situation was stabilised. It was a very anxious time. We were digging back lines to defend the Channel Ports. We had to leave Cassel, except as an advanced H.Q., and move to Blendecque, near St. Omer. Hazebrouck was threatened, and the enemy reached Strazeele. Our hopes of stemming the tide rested on the arrival of an Australian division under Major-General Walker. We had officers and men from our schools, servants, grooms, etc., all in the line.

The trains bringing the Australians were four hours late, I met them at Hazebrouck and how glad I was to see them. They went straight into action and drove the enemy from Strazeele and Flêtre. That was the end; the enemy had shot his bolt. It had been a very trying month. The work of those tired and weakened divisions was heroic and undoubtedly saved the Channel Ports. The Belgians on our left deserve great credit; they would not yield a yard.

I look back on those days from April 8th, when the attack developed on us, as the worst I remember in the war. It seemed so terrible to give up all that we had fought for and gained. One could see and feel that the net was closing round us. I remember General Hunter Weston, who was holding Passchendaele, coming to tell me how serious the situation was there, and it fell to me to suggest to the army commander that we must consider giving it up, and I well remember his answer: "I won't have it."

A little later he came down to my room and said: "You were right, issue the orders." It was a very trying moment. I issued the orders, and later on the dear old chief came down again and said: "Have the orders gone out?" They had, but there was that great stout old heart having a last struggle to hold on. It had to be the risk was too great; our position was impossible. That withdrawal was carried out in the most perfect order. Our line was withdrawn in the night to the outskirts of Ypres. Thank God we never lost Ypres itself.

After the move of the British Army to the north at the end of 1914, I was connected with the defence of the Ypres Salient except for four months in Italy, until I came home in May 1918. I served nowhere else. I knew it with the 49th Division, Canadian Corps, and I knew it with the Second Army. It was a terrible problem, and it was fortunate that in the man who bore that responsibility we had one with an extra stout heart.

How well I remember that old road from Poperinghe to Ypres—the bravery of those transport drivers who took supplies in and through Ypres, where out casualties were often 100 per night. The dodging through Ypres at night and in the early hours. That run to Hell Fire Corner and beyond. There were some terrible places all marked down by the enemy. The officers and men who held that Salient were indeed heroes; they faced death at every hour of the day and night. Nothing could break their great spirit, any more than it could break the spirit of that wonderful wounded pigeon, which I remember at the loft behind Poperinghe, when it laid down its message and died, its duty nobly done.

On May 8th, 1918, to my great regret, I left the Second Army and ended my happy association with my old chief. He was like a father to me. We had been together for two years, through good and bad times, in the defence of the Ypres Salient. It was a great privilege and education to serve under a chief like him— so thoughtful for those under him, so human, so thorough, so determined to give himself and to get the best out of everyone under him—always the same, always cheerful and full of humour. He was at his best when things were difficult or not going well. Always so generous to others, he never wished to take any credit, but always to give it to his staff. He had an amazing power of attraction.

I have in my possession two most wonderful letters, one of which he sent to me the morning after the Battle of Messines, and the other the day I left. He was so moved on such occasions that he was unable to speak. I treasure those two letters deeply. They are not letters for publication. I have tried so hard, in the twenty years of command which I have had since I left him, to follow his methods, and I have so often said to myself: "Now what would the old chief have done?" It has been a great help, but he had some extra bit somewhere that the rest of us cannot get.

As I walked in his funeral procession, from the Guards Chapel to Westminster Abbey, carrying his orders and decorations, I could see very many old soldiers with tears in their eyes, obviously men who had served under the old chief in various parts of the world. He was buried in the Warriors' Chapel, and each year, on the anniversary of the Battle of Messines, it has been our privilege to place flowers on his grave.

I have visited the old Salient several times since the Great War. I unveiled a tablet in the cathedral on one occasion, and I attended with Lord Plumer when he unveiled the Memorial to the Missing at the Menin Gate. The Mayor of Ypres was ill, and the late King of the Belgians, who was leading the procession, stopped at his house and went in to see him. I think that ceremony was by far the most impressive I ever attended. I described it fully in my *Life of Lord Plumer*, so I will not repeat it, but his rendering of "He is not missing, he is here," will long be remembered by all who heard him.

The British School at Ypres, chiefly attended by children of those who look after war graves with such care, the little British Church in which Lord Plumer's G.C.B. Banner is laid up, all bring back those days—also the Canadian War Memorial near Mt. Sorrel, the beautiful Tyne Cot Cemetery, in which I once met fifty Germans on a bicycle tour—I know no more wonderful or impressive place than this cemetery; when I was C.-in-C. at Aldershot I tried to reproduce it at the *Finale* of the Tattoo, but it was too difficult. In the darkest days of September, 1938, in Gibraltar, I was always hopeful, and always comforted by the belief that those represented by the million little white crosses, who died for us, did not give their lives in vain.

Through all the anxious months of 1939 up to 3rd September, I always held that hope, I prayed earnestly that we might be spared the horrors of another war. God knows every possible effort was made by our Prime Minister, Lord Halifax and others to prevent it, but to no avail.

We of the older generation never thought to see our country plunged into war again.

Twenty-one years ago, (as of 1940), we never thought it would be possible during our lifetime for our former enemy again to get into position to embark on another war, nor did we think it would be even possible for one man to gain a position from which he could defy the world. Yet such has happened.

I think that I am justly entitled to regard myself as the last link of the old Second Army. Recent events have hit one very hard. We never thought that our old Ypres Salient would be overrun, and so easily, by those whom we had kept at bay with British pluck and lives for four years. Our beloved Messines Ridge, Mt. Kemmel, Mt. des Cats, Sherpenberg, Poperinghe, Hazebrouck, Cassel, Elverdinghe, Brieleu, St. Eloi, Hill 60, and Ypres itself—all gone and battered to pieces.

I have talked with soldiers who recently came through those hallowed places *en route* to Dunkirk. Our old Toc H House at Poperinghe, which Lord Wakefield had generously restored for us, is flat. The Upper Room in which so many great men in the last war took their last communion has gone. The old carpenter's bench at which that communion was administered had been previously removed to the cellars below so may be yet preserved.

I suppose the little British church and British school at Ypres have also been destroyed. I understand that the gardeners—the men who have so faithfully guarded the memory of those millions who died for us—were all safely evacuated. The link with the old Second Army has been broken and broken by the son of the gallant king and soldier for whom we gave those British lives. It is a mercy that he has been spared the disgrace brought on his army by his own son. But for that monstrous act of treachery, the war would have taken a very different course, and in my opinion, we should still be in possession of the old and hallowed places which I have referred to above.

D.C.I.G.S.

It was on May 8th, that I reached London and joined Sir Henry Wilson as D.C.I.G.S. No one was more surprised than I was. I had known of it for some time, but after the German attack of March 21st, on the Third and Fifth Armies, the Germans turned on the Second Army in the north, where we had very severe fighting, losing Passchendaele, Kemmel, Messines, Bailleul, etc., and it was not until May 8th that the situation was stabilized and the German advance brought to a standstill. During all this time Henry Wilson had kept the appointment open for me.

I always remember the first question I was asked on the day I arrived (one which I knew was being discussed at the time). Did I recommend that Haig should be replaced by my old chief, Plumer? An awkward question, when still in my pocket was the precious letter that my old chief had given me that morning because he was too moved to speak. However, I had no hesitation in saying definitely "No." To lose Haig at that moment when the situation had been definitely stabilised would have shaken the British Army from top to bottom. I told Lord Plumer later of this conversation and of my reply. All he said was: "Naturally; you would have got yourself into trouble if you hadn't."

I had just finished a unique education of two and a half years with Lord Plumer in the defence of the Ypres Salient, and I was now to start on another two and a half years under quite different circumstances.

I am now going to tell my readers something about this

very remarkable, and most ill-judged man, Henry Wilson, with whom I had the closest association through a very difficult time. I am going to write quite frankly about him, for I knew him really well, and many who have criticized him never knew him at all. How I wish that I could give my readers a true picture of this great man! He had an amazing and most attractive personality, a wonderful sense of humour, a love of fun and children, and a wonderful, kind heart. He had a marvellously quick brain, and it was almost uncanny what he saw.

He was at school at Marlborough. He had, he always said, a job to get into the army; eventually he succeeded through the Longford Militia. He loved the regimental life in India and Burma, where he was unfortunately wounded. By this time, he had evidently decided to take soldiering seriously. It was curious to think that in 1891, he was able to pass into the Staff College only seven years after he had been struggling to get into the army at all.

His work at the Staff College and his subsequent staff appointments, leading up to the post of Assistant Military Secretary to Lord Roberts, with whom he returned to England after the South African War, all go to show how highly he was thought of. By his determined efforts to lay the foundation of an efficient general staff he was selected to be *commandant* of the Staff College in January, 1907, and I was privileged to be a student under him. Those of us who had that privilege will never forget those days—the interesting schemes; the trips to the 1,870 battlefields; the Mountain Warfare scheme, when we almost ran up Snowdon; joint schemes with the navy, etc.

It was during this time that he began his great friendship with Foch which, in later years when he was D.M.O., was to mean so much in formulating the plans between the French and British Staffs before the Great War. He was branded as "All French", but, I ask, where should we have been without those detailed plans? We owe a deep debt to the men who made them so perfect. Marshal Foch always said that Henry Wilson was the only Englishman who understood the French, but, as I know better than others, he did not hesitate to blame the French on many occasions when he did not think they had played their part.

At the time of the Ulster crisis in the spring of 1914, I was serving under Henry Wilson; I was attached from Aldershot, revising the Field Service Regulations. Those were very difficult days, especially for Irishmen. Henry Wilson, a devout Ulsterman and Protestant, did what he thought was right. He played a big part, quite oblivious of the consequences to himself. The crisis eventually passed but, in certain quarters, Henry Wilson was never forgiven. I think that the reason he was never allowed to be C.G.S. to Sir John French, who asked for him when Sir A. Murray went Home to the War Office, was on account of his recent activities over Ulster. In addition, he did not see eye to eye with Lord Kitchener; they were two men of such different temperaments.

After leaving G.H.Q., Henry Wilson commanded the IV Corps for a time, but I never think that this was his line. His brain, and grasp of the world problem, was being wasted by the narrow vision of trench warfare. People used to say that he never understood the regimental soldier, and that he lived in a cloud. It is totally untrue. How often he used to say to me: "Gosh, what would the regimental officer or soldier think of that sort of order:" He never for a moment forgot their point of view. His trouble was that he saw a great deal further than his critics.

When he completed his term as C.I.G.S., the War Office put all the papers which he had prepared for the Cabinet, on every theatre of war and country, into book form, and they gave me, as his deputy, a copy which I have today. He said to me once: "It' is uncanny what I see." So true—I often look through those papers after all these years. His prophecies were uncanny. His grasp of the situation in all our seven theatres of war, and in the world generally, was wonderful.

On one occasion when he gave a lecture to the Cabinet and to all the Dominion Premiers in his room at the War Office, Mr. Lloyd George gave orders that no soldiers were to be present. The D.M.O., Major-General P. de B. Radcliffe, was very disappointed, and so was I, but when all the maps were suitably arranged, I asked if there was anything more I could do, and retired. All eyes were on the lecturer, so I shut the door firmly, myself inside, and I hid on the floor behind the last row! When the lecture ended, I opened the door from the inside but was never caught. It was a wonderful lecture and I had no intention of missing it!

After the IV Corps various jobs were found for Henry Wilson: his mission to Russia; liaison with General Nivelle; the Eastern Command; the visit to Italy after Caporetto, where Lord Plumer and I met him with Foch, Weygand and others; the famous Doullens Conference, where we met him again, at which Haig so generously and loyally agreed that the Allied Command should be given to Marshal Foch; and eventually the Supreme War Council at Versailles.

In February, 1918, he became C.I.G.S. in place of Sir William Robertson. As one looks back and reads in his own diaries and in other books, one cannot fail to be struck by the great and important part this soldier was playing. He was the only soldier who knew the political leaders; he knew them all well and was certainly not afraid to speak his mind. Mr. Lloyd George, Mr. Winston Churchill—all believed in him then and appreciated his quick vision. He was quite the opposite to the usual slow and cautious soldier when confronted with leading politicians at a Cabinet Meeting.

Believe me or not, Henry Wilson cared nothing for self, he had only one purpose and that was to win the war. Jealousies were bound to come in. I deplore all the difficulties, changes, political strifes, political moves, strategical ideas, Western and Eastern parties which seem to have been rife at that time. The truth is that there were three brains which worked about twice as fast as any others—Lloyd George, Winston Churchill and Henry Wilson—all three were determined to win the war.

Henry Wilson often made enemies through people not understanding his chaff. Haig did not like him; his brain was too quick for Haig. Robertson never liked him, and General Archie

Murray, who was C.G.S. at the start of the war, disliked him intensely. But he hated having enemies and would go to any length to be friends.

On the eve of going to France in August, 1914, he went over to the Admiralty to make up a quarrel with his old friend Mr. Winston Churchill. He told me that he had been worried by this difference of opinion (presumably over Ireland) for some time, and felt that he could not go to France with it on his mind. I believe they shook hands and made it up and were both much moved.

When, just after the war, he returned from staying with Mr. Lloyd George (in those days they were great friends), I remember so well his saying to me: "Tim, I was sitting on the little man's bed last night and he told me that though he had worked hard to win the war, he had nothing by which to remember it, and he asked me if I thought it would be nice to ask the king to give him a D.C.M. as a souvenir, to which I agreed." The king did not agree, but gave him an O.M. (Order of Merit). What a tragedy those friendships broke down!

When I came Home as D.C.I.G.S., Sir William Robertson was at the Horse Guards as C.-in-C. Home Forces. There had been differences, and this seemed to me a pity at this stage; it seemed to be bad for the country. I sounded Sir Henry Wilson, who told me that he wanted to have no differences and only wanted to be friends, so I got Sir William Robertson to agree and arranged a meeting over something to do with Home Defence. Sir Henry Wilson said he was quite ready to go over to the Horse Guards to save Sir William Robertson trouble.

That meeting I shall never forget. We went over together and, after waiting some time, were shown into Sir William's room in the Horse Guards. I saw from the start that it was going to be difficult. I do not think they had discussed much, if anything at all, when an orderly came in and said: "Your tea, sir?" Sir William said: "Yes," and the orderly brought in his tea, which he drank as we sat there. It was a pity, and we soon left. I had thought that I was doing a good deed. I got into awful trouble from Lady

Wilson for my action.

As D.C.I.G.S. my job was entirely confined to the army. I had nothing of any kind to do with politics. Having been associated with Henry Wilson, naturally I have ever since been tarred with the same brush, but it only amuses me. So little do I care about politics that only once in my life have I had a vote; that was when I lived near Pinner some years before the war. I went to hear each candidate speak. As neither said one word about the defence of the Empire I never voted for either, and I should do exactly the same tomorrow. I think that is why, in later years, I managed to get on with both Greeks and Turks in Constantinople; and with both sides in Spain. I am pro-nothing except pro-English.

I used to attend Cabinet meetings nearly every day; one of us had to be there to give the military situation in various theatres of war. I met all the members of the Cabinet, who were very kind to me. It was a great education. Mr. Lloyd George was kind until one day about July, 1918. Marshal Foch had asked for a scheme to provide 5,000 tanks and 10,000 tractors to win the war on a 100-mile front in 1919 or 1920. I had, in conjunction with the D.M.O., Major-General Radcliffe, prepared a paper on the subject for the C.I.G.S. for discussion by the Cabinet. I attended the Cabinet with Lord Milner, Secretary for State, and the C.I.G.S. It was a full Cabinet meeting with all the Dominion Prime Ministers present. Mr. Lloyd George opened the proceedings by taking Item 5 first, the General Staff paper. He turned to me and said: "You wrote this, didn't you?"

I replied that I had had something to do with it. He then said: "What's it going to cost?" and I replied that I had no idea, when he suddenly turned on me and said: "You are just like all these soldiers, you never think about men's lives." As I had just returned from nearly four years connected with the defence of the Ypres Salient, I thought a good deal about men's lives, and as the project under discussion did not envisage either the year, or the theatre of war, it was a little difficult to calculate the cost in men's lives.

At first, in fact, I had thought he had meant the cost in money. I own to being very angry, but on the way back to the War Office, arm in arm with Henry Wilson, the latter told me that I must not mind, as it was all done for effect; that Mr. Lloyd George had chosen me to bully as I was the junior, and it was really to impress the Colonial Premiers and to show them the way he dealt with soldiers. Then he added: "There is that little man; he is out to win the war if it takes another twenty years, and he will always give you a decision when no one else will." Very true. I bear Mr. Lloyd George no grudge for those days; he was wonderful; though he killed me later over Chanak, or nearly so.

The other military members of the Army Council were Sir John Cowans, Sir Nevil Macready, Sir William Furse and, later, Sir John Du Cane, M.G.O. All these were much senior to me, but as general staff officer, in the absence of Sir Henry Wilson, I had to preside at the military meetings daily, and often twice a day, and I shall never forget their kindness to me. Those were indeed busy days; I seldom left the War Office before 9 p.m. and seldom got to bed before 2 a.m.

Those months from May till the Armistice were full of interest. The combing out by Auckland Geddes: the cry for more men: Rawlinson's attack on 8th August; I was actually at a Cabinet meeting when news of that success came in. The Australian Premier was very angry at the Australians being employed without his knowledge, but when he heard of their success, he struck quite a different tune. I also remember Lloyd George's annoyance at four British divisions being ordered south by Foch to help the French. General Smuts and the D.M.O., P. de B. Radcliffe were sent to France to protest, but Haig had known all the time that an attack was coming in that region and had willingly agreed.

At long last the enemy resistance broke. How well do I remember the telegrams coming in from all the theatres of war, leading up to that great 11th November, 1918. At 12 noon that day the Army Council proceeded to Buckingham Palace and were received by the king and queen and taken out on to the balcony to see that wonderful scene of thousands and thousands of devoted and thankful subjects—a scene one can never forget.

LEONAUR

ALSO FROM LEONAUR
AVAILABLE IN SOFTCOVER OR HARDCOVER WITH DUST JACKET

THE WOMAN IN BATTLE *by Loreta Janeta Velazquez*—Soldier, Spy and Secret Service Agent for the Confederacy During the American Civil War.

BOOTS AND SADDLES *by Elizabeth B. Custer*—The experiences of General Custer's Wife on the Western Plains.

FANNIE BEERS' CIVIL WAR *by Fannie A. Beers*—A Confederate Lady's Experiences of Nursing During the Campaigns & Battles of the American Civil War.

LADY SALE'S AFGHANISTAN *by Florentia Sale*—An Indomitable Victorian Lady's Account of the Retreat from Kabul During the First Afghan War.

THE TWO WARS OF MRS DUBERLY *by Frances Isabella Duberly*—An Intrepid Victorian Lady's Experience of the Crimea and Indian Mutiny.

THE REBELLIOUS DUCHESS *by Paul F. S. Dermoncourt*—The Adventures of the Duchess of Berri and Her Attempt to Overthrow French Monarchy.

LADIES OF WATERLOO *by Charlotte A. Eaton, Magdalene de Lancey & Juana Smith*—The Experiences of Three Women During the Campaign of 1815: Waterloo Days by Charlotte A. Eaton, A Week at Waterloo by Magdalene de Lancey & Juana's Story by Juana Smith.

NURSE AND SPY IN THE UNION ARMY *by Sarah Emma Evelyn Edmonds*—During the American Civil War

WIFE NO. 19 *by Ann Eliza Young*—The Life & Ordeals of a Mormon Woman During the 19th Century

DIARY OF A NURSE IN SOUTH AFRICA *by Alice Bron*—With the Dutch-Belgian Red Cross During the Boer War

MARIE ANTOINETTE AND THE DOWNFALL OF ROYALTY *by Imbert de Saint-Amand*—The Queen of France and the French Revolution

THE MEMSAHIB & THE MUTINY *by R. M. Coopland*—An English lady's ordeals in Gwalior and Agra duringthe Indian Mutiny 1857

MY CAPTIVITY AMONG THE SIOUX INDIANS *by Fanny Kelly*—The ordeal of a pioneer woman crossing the Western Plains in 1864

WITH MAXIMILIAN IN MEXICO *by Sara Yorke Stevenson*—A Lady's experience of the French Adventure

www.ingramcontent.com/pod-product-compliance
Lightning Source LLC
Chambersburg PA
CBHW032057080426
42733CB00006B/315